From **RAGS**

to *Wishes* !

Oli
You Are the Best !
Get Jiggle Wizzo
W/ Io It !!!

From RAGS to *Wishes*

The Naked Truth about Turning
Failure into Fortune

Van Allen

Brown Books Publishing Group
Dallas, Texas

From Rags to Wishes
The Naked Truth about Turning Failure into Fortune
© 2010 Van Allen

Manufactured in the United States of America.

Brown Books Publishing Group
16200 North Dallas Parkway, Suite 170
Dallas, Texas 75248
www.brownbooks.com
972-381-0009

A New Era in Publishing™

ISBN-13: 978-1-934812-61-7
ISBN-10: 1-934812-61-7

LCCN: 2010920707
1 2 3 4 5 6 7 8 9 10

To everyone who is committed to helping
people get what they want out of life.

To everyone who accepts the premise that we
were not put on this earth to realize only our goals but to
help a whole bunch of other people realize theirs.

To those who have had an impact on my life and
encouraged me every step of the way to stay in the game,
especially my wife, daughter, and parents.

Contents

Acknowledgments

First, I want to thank the two people in my life who make me feel everyday as if I hung the moon and the stars. They have to put up with someone who is a mad scientist with ideas and can be quite moody at times while I try and figure things out. They give me the space to think and support all of my endeavors, even when they don't work out as planned. Julie, my wife, and Reagan, my daughter, are my inspiration and the reason I get out of bed every day and do it all over again. I'm glad you guys love amusements parks because this roller coaster is quite a ride. I love you two.

I want to thank my folks, John and Carolyn Allen, for letting me come into this world. You couldn't ask for better parents. Tough love, vinyl belts, and a whole bunch of hugging is what they provided, and it served as the foundation to my journey. You guys are simply the best. I love you Mom and Dad.

I want to thank my two siblings, Barry and Beau, who will always be my two best friends in the world. They have watched and endured all of my wackiness throughout the years and never discouraged me from turning over another stone and giving it another shot. Barry's wife, Bronwyn, has also been there for me, providing encouragement and guidance for over twenty years. Thanks. Oh yeah, and she taught me how to dance and do the Bus Driver.

I have to say thanks to the guys who have golfed with me over the years and have been my outlet for extreme laughter, craziness, friendly wagering, and a lot of encouraging words:

- Mike Flanagan (Triangle, Serenity Now)
- Ed Orr (185, Right down the middle)
- Scotty McDaniel ("Did anyone see that? How can that ball not break")
- Brad Dixon (4 Birdies pays $100.00)
- Richard Vairo ("Don't worry about it; there's always a buy down at the end")
- Jonathan Tips ("All right now")
- Tommy Darrough ("Talking Tommy: that's my best shot ever")
- Kevin Adam, one of my closest buddies who is always there for me ("Just add one more loop and give me a little more kitty litter")

Thanks to all of you and HAMMER!!!

Author's Note

I started TimeLine Recruiting, a physician recruiting firm, in May 1999 with one employee, me, and I sold the company six years later for millions. People occasionally ask how I did it. Or they might ask me to share my business model or strategies or guiding principles. What they're really asking is will I share the secret. Will I share the keys to my success and in doing so give them an outline for building their own successful organizations? For those with the patience or the interest, the answer to all these questions is the book you hold in your hands.

From Rags to Wishes: The Naked Truth about Turning Failure into Fortune is a rags-to-riches story, and I'm happy to share it, warts and all. Along the way I made mistakes. More than I should have. More, in fact, than I thought possible for one man to make in a lifetime. I'm willing to share those mistakes because in these missteps and bad decisions I found the path to my own success. I'm tempted to tell you that, like me, you too have to make mistakes, that wrong-headed thinking and the painful events that follow hold the keys to success, but it's not true. And don't let anyone tell you that mistakes, in and of themselves, build character, organizations, or value. What builds character, organizations, and value is learning from your mistakes.

My path to building an exceptional organizational culture, to profitability, and to a cash sale for millions had to do with applying a set of sound business principles that I had to learn for myself. Some of those include demonstrating flagrant honesty, accepting that belief is contagious, making a great product, changing behaviors by giving options, and understanding that success is fragile. I'm willing to share these lessons and, in most cases, the sometimes embarrassing stories and events that drove the principles home because I wish someone had shared these principles with me.

Mine is a first-hand story of early success, hitting bottom, surviving, and finally prospering. Of the thousands of recruiting companies across the nation, only a handful achieved the success TimeLine Recruiting achieved in my brief tenure as CEO. Whatever your industry and whatever your product or service, I'm here to tell you that if I can lead an organization to this level of success, you can too.

ONE

● ● ● ● ● ● ● ● ●

Flagrant Honesty

Honesty is the first chapter in the book of wisdom.
—*Thomas Jefferson*

Honesty is good for business. Flagrant honesty is even better. Many burgeoning businesses focus on only one goal—survival. Yet I would suggest an equally important business principle—flagrant honesty. The word *flagrant* may sound odd in this context, but I use it here to express a glaring and conspicuous honesty. I'm not just referring to telling the truth but telling the entire truth and the context and the possible outcomes of those truths. The word usually applies to errors, as in "a flagrant mistake," but it equally applies to any burning and passionate action, like telling the truth.

In the early days of a new business, nothing is more important than establishing the values that will guide your company through growth to success. What better value to serve as the cornerstone of your business than flagrant honesty. It's all too easy to over-promise, to compromise your principles, to misrepresent financial statements and other dishonest acts to get that first big deal, but in the end, those decisions can destroy a company. Follow a policy of flagrant honesty, on the other hand, and you have laid a foundation of trust that clients will be drawn to intuitively.

I started TimeLine Recruiting in May 1999. In October, a buddy from grad school, David Wright, called and asked if I was interested in recruiting several doctors for the company he worked for, ProMedCo Management Company, a physician practice management firm. He said they needed as many qualified physicians as I could find. And he needed them fast. I explained that I had just opened my doors, but David insisted I send over a proposal. He'd offered me a pot of gold, yet I wasn't sure I was ready for it. In effect, I tried to convince him I wasn't the right guy for the job. I told him I didn't have letterhead. I didn't have business cards. I didn't have an office. I didn't have anything. He wasn't buying it and suggested I talk with Debbie, the person responsible for physician recruitment at ProMedCo. I called Debbie knowing it was a long shot. In fact, I called mostly out of respect for David. At the time, I had only one client, a small hospital in Mexico, Missouri, which had retained me to find an anesthesiologist.

I called Debbie and introduced myself. She gave me some background on the organization and outlined their needs. She asked me to send over a bid with my fees and deliverables. I'd ordered letterhead from the printer, but it hadn't arrived. I could wait and kill a few days, or I could type up a proposal without the letterhead. This was 1999, and I'd just bought my first personal computer, a laptop I didn't know how to operate. Today it sounds silly, but in those days using a laptop was, for me at least, a monumental task. I didn't know the first thing about personal computers or word processing or printers or printer drivers or anything else related to computers.

What the heck. David had asked for a proposal, and I'd committed to delivering one. I handwrote my proposal to

ProMedCo. I gave my fees and deliverables for two physician searches. David needed more than two doctors, but I could effectively handle the two searches on my own. Once I filled the two searches, I'd ask for more business. I signed it and faxed the proposal to Debbie within the hour.

Three days passed, and Debbie called and said I won the contract. ProMedCo had fired their previous physician recruiting firm, and she wanted to make sure I understood their needs. She said, "If you could put a contract together for thirty searches, we can get this thing going."

"Debbie," I said, "I've got to be honest with you. I can't commit to thirty searches. It's just me. I can do three or four searches. But until I hire some staff, I can't handle thirty."

"Three or four searches?" she said, and I could hear the frustration in her voice. I got off the phone, and I started calling everybody I knew who might have an interest in getting into the physician recruiting business. I hired two people overnight and started training the following day. I called Debbie back and told her I'd take ten searches. For a budding recruiting company, taking on ten searches was huge. My fee was $2,000 a month per search, which meant my small company had gone from $2,000 a month in revenue from my one client to $22,000 a month overnight. My contract was a five-month commitment—$2,000 per month times ten searches times five months came to $100,000 in revenue. I also earned revenue on outgoing direct mail campaigns designed to get doctors to call our office and discuss the opportunity plus a bonus for each doctor who accepted the job.

Winning a contract for ten searches was a bonanza. Sure, I could have taken twenty or even all thirty searches. I could have run down to a printer and cranked out a rush letterhead to make me look good. I could have hidden the fact that I was small and had just started the company. I could have done a lot of things, but I opted not to do any of those, and that contract for ten searches turned into twenty and then into thirty.

I believe the reason ProMedCo continually gave me more business was twofold: I told the truth, and the high quality of my work on the searches was evident. I was a straightforward guy who said, "You know, I can get your job done, but I can't do everything."

I was starting a company, and the last thing I wanted was to underperform. ProMedCo was one of the biggest Physician Practice Management Companies (PPMCs) in the country, and I wanted to build a strong reputation, and that reputation was worth more than just revenue.

You don't really know you're honest until you're tempted. Isn't that true? It's easy to take a moral stand when there are no other options. In this instance there was a lot of money on the table, and I took only a small piece of it because in taking that small piece I was able to guarantee the quality of my service and build my reputation based on that quality.

In that moment, I learned I was an honest person. I didn't lie. I didn't even scramble for ways to look like something I wasn't, to appear larger and more polished, and that honesty paid off. Had Debbie heard something in my presentation that impressed her? I think it was candor. I was honest about the facts, honest about what I could and couldn't do. That honesty was effective. You may think you need hype to succeed, right? Well, you don't.

Sometimes you can win a big contract or close a big deal with the glitz. Sure you can. But over the long term, people want honesty. ProMedCo had just fired one of the most well-respected recruiting firms in the country, Merritt Hawkins. I know; I used to work for them. Merritt Hawkins was large and polished and had impressive marketing materials. I knew I couldn't compete on size and experience and sparkle. I had to come up with an approach to level the playing field. My approach was to be honest. Debbie heard honesty. She heard I was willing to lose the business.

What do we usually hear when a salesman calls on the phone? Desperation. Need. Greed. What did Debbie hear? She heard a willingness to help, a willingness to lend a hand with her and her needs. She heard sincerity. She heard good will. She heard, "I'm going to give you everything I've got. It may not meet your needs and I want to be honest about that, but you'll get my best." And that must have been the most unusual thing she heard from all the people and companies who submitted a proposal.

That simple message was extremely powerful.

As my business grew, I used to tell clients, "You know what? There is a chance I'm not going to fill your search. But let me tell what you're going to get," and I'd list the tangible and intangible results of my efforts. I'd list the tasks, obligations, and purpose of my work effort to find qualified physicians and recruit them to work for my clients. In short, I didn't promise what I couldn't deliver.

How do you cut though the noise in a world filled with hype and unfulfilled promises? Flagrant honesty. Give your clients, and your employees, flagrant honesty and you'll stand out from the crowd. You'll win the business. It doesn't matter how big the other guy is or how many competitors you have. Nobody in today's highly competitive marketplace is playing that card. I never tried to be something I wasn't, and you shouldn't either.

Flagrant honesty is rare, and people will pay for what's rare. If you have something that's rare, you have no competition. Where is flagrant honesty today? Nowhere. You need courage to be honest. You need courage when you're earning $2,000 a month and a client offers you a pot of gold and you know in your heart you can't deliver if you say yes. It takes courage to be flagrantly honest. She heard honesty and courage, and she bought it.

A Little Back Story

One day in 1993, I came across a classified ad for a search consultant with Merritt Hawkins & Associates, the nation's largest physician placement company. I didn't know what a search consultant did exactly, but I called, interviewed, and got the job. Landing that job became the foundation for the company I eventually built and sold for millions several years later. I cut my teeth in recruiting doctors at Merritt Hawkins, and for that I'll always be thankful to those who gave me a chance.

I immersed myself in the industry. I learned the nuances of the health care world, the complexities, and the overall structure of hiring and retaining doctors. I spent the better part of five years at Merritt Hawkins learning the industry inside and out. At the same time, I began graduate school at night with a focus on health services management. With about a semester to go, I received a call from Bruce Eady, CEO of Columbia Regional Hospital, one of many hospitals owned by Tenet Healthcare Corporation.

I'd first met Bruce when I began recruiting doctors for Columbia Regional. He desperately needed a highly competent executive to oversee thirteen clinics connected to the hospital. Bruce was a pretty good negotiator himself, and he knew what motivated me. "I need someone good," he said, "and I thought of you."

Bruce Eady had me. In one respect, accepting the job was a difficult decision. I loved Merritt Hawkins. The company had been good to me, and it was a great company to work for. I was very successful there, reaching a height few accomplished. I left on good terms, partly because I would now be managing health care clinics and therefore become a client. Clinics, like hospitals, need qualified doctors, and who else would I choose to recruit for me? I envisioned a close and ongoing relationship with my former company.

When I arrived in Columbia, I learned why Bruce was desperate for help. The clinics were a mess—poor management, mediocre quality, low patient satisfaction numbers, long wait times, careless follow-up procedures, lax controls, billing errors, and lousy employee morale. By any measure, the clinics were underperforming. I'd walked into a business with no organizational discipline where physicians were free to create their own private fiefdoms.

In March, barely four months after beginning work at Columbia Regional, Bruce Eady called and asked me to join him and seven others on his executive team for lunch at Chris McDee's, a dark and moody restaurant on the south side of town. The group lunch was unplanned and out of character with Bruce's more typical "let's all meet in the conference room" approach. I arrived and squeezed myself up to the already crowded table. Bruce sat at the head of the table and raised his glass. "To our time together," Bruce said and downed half his drink. He placed his glass on the table and glanced at each of us. "Go on. Drink up. After what I'm about to say, you'll need it."

"What's going on?" I asked.

"Columbia Regional Hospital is on the chopping block."

"Meaning?"

"I wanted to give you a heads up. Tonight at 5 PM there's going to be a public announcement. Tenet Healthcare Corporation is selling our hospital to the University. Thereafter, most of you will be employed by the University of Missouri."

"You said most of us," I said.

Bruce brushed lint from his blue suit with the narrow lapels. He reached for his drink, lifted it, and changed his mind and set it down again. "I'm sorry, Van. There's nothing for you here."

For a moment, I went numb. I'd just quit a great job where I was happy and made great money. I took a pay cut to expand my knowledge and my professional base as a health care professional. I pushed my chair back from the table and felt sick to my stomach.

"Who else?" one of the men at the table asked.

"Who else what?" Bruce said.

"Who else is fired?"

"Not fired. I never said fired. We're moving some people around is all. I'd like to meet with each of you. Later today, if you have time. We can go over all your questions in private. There's much work to do."

As for my job, I wasn't fired. Not exactly. Management of the clinics and other systems was being relocated to Philadelphia, and I could come along if I wanted. The job was put to me with just about that much enthusiasm. "You can come along if you want." That wasn't going to happen. I wasn't moving for a variety of reasons. I'd met a woman, Julie, and fallen in love in the span of a few weeks. We later married, but at the time, we were awash in the euphoria of early romance. Julie graduated from the University of Missouri located right there in Columbia, and she loved it here. She knew a lot of people in the area and had family nearby. As for me, I was tired of moving. I was starting to like small town living.

I remember how uneasy I was that evening after the meeting. Julie and I had planned a night out, and my job was to retell the bad news. We sat close together in a booth in a posh restaurant with a white tablecloth, white napkins, and bone-white dishes. The setting was much like the table earlier that afternoon.

I sipped my drink. "I'm out of a job," I said. "I'm unemployed, and there's nothing for me to do here in Columbia."

"What are you going to do? Before you answer, let me ask what you want to do."

"Tenet has asked me to move to Philadelphia. They just bought the bankrupt Allegheny Health System there in western

Pennsylvania. They've invited me to come work with the clinics."

"I asked what you want to do."

"I'm not sure how to answer that."

She leaned forward and aligned her silverware. She tapped at the base of a wine glass with her finger and took a deep breath. Softly, she said, "I'm not moving to Philadelphia."

"If you're not moving and I can't find a job here, what do we do?"

"Why don't you start your own company?"

I could hear the voices of diners around us, a feathery laugh, a man telling a joke, a waiter describing a pricey Cabernet. "I know recruiting. Physician recruiting, I mean. It's a specialized field. There's a ton of competition, but the only type of recruiting company I would have is a retained recruiting company. They are virtually impossible to start because you can't get any of the business. It's a very small niche market, and everyone I know who has tried to start a recruiting company has fallen flat."

"And?"

"It's expensive. I'd need capital. I don't have any money. You know that. I'm broke or at least broke from the standpoint of starting a company."

Julie glanced at her menu and looked at me. "How much do you need?"

I explained I'd probably need about $15,000, but even that was a wild guess. As I talked, listing off rent and computer equipment and phone systems and supplies and whatever popped into my head, this woman I'd been dating for all of six weeks pulled out her checkbook and wrote me a check for $15,000. I stopped talking, and she placed her fingers on the edge of the check and slid the paper in front of me. I stared at it, mute.

"There you go," she said.

"I can't take it."

"Van, whether we get married, whether this thing lasts another two months, two years, or two decades, you need to start a company. We've talked about this. It's what you want whether you know it or not."

"Julie, how am I going to pay this back?"

"You're going to make money, right?" She dropped her pen into the checkbook and purposefully closed her checkbook into her purse. "Now," she said, "let's have dinner."

And we did.

TWO

● ● ● ● ● ● ● ● ●

Believing Is Contagious

The thing always happens that you really believe in,
and the belief in a thing makes it happen.
—Frank Lloyd Wright

Belief can make a good business better and a better business great. Yet belief as a business principle is often overlooked by business leaders precisely because it is intangible. You and I can't touch it or feel it. We can't measure it in any quantifiable way. Nonetheless, I suggest there is a direct correlation between belief and improved profits, innovative products, better customer service, and happier employees. Belief is the habit of placing trust in yourself and in others. It's more than attitude; it's a conviction in the truth. The power of belief can be applied to many aspects of your business—mission, strategy, products, services, customers, clients, and your ability to market and sell.

When you most need to believe isn't when you have a stellar product or a breakthrough process or a willing client. Belief is much less important when things are going your way. You need to believe when the deck is stacked against you—your sales team can't close a sale, your processes are breaking down, your clients are making unreasonable demands, or your prospects have unrealistic expectations. When you face these obstacles, the solution isn't to hire new staff, invent a new process, or find new clients. The solution is to believe in yourself, your values, and your mission because when you believe enough, those beliefs become contagious.

Believe and those around you will believe. Those around you influence the organization, and the organization influences your customers and clients. If you want to sell something nobody wants or at least doesn't know he wants, what do you need to do? You need to think and behave in ways that demonstrate your conviction. You need to trust in your belief forming processes and take action consistent with those beliefs. Do all this, and you can sell anything. You just need to believe. It is contagious, and you need staff who get infected.

Nowhere is belief more critical to the growth of your company than in the recruiting business. Most recruiting firms are paid once the doctor accepts a position with the hospital. TimeLine was different. We worked on a retainer, much like a lawyer or an accountant, which meant the hospital paid us before we located a physician. Of the fifteen hundred physician recruiting firms in the country, less than eight are exclusively retained recruiting companies like TimeLine. There are so few because our search services are a hard sell; I was asking CEOs and clinic administrators to hand over a $40,000 check long before they saw any results.

To get a single appointment with a CEO, I'd spend days calling hospitals in small towns across the Midwest. In the early years, once I got an appointment, I'd climb into my five-year-old, front wheel drive, not-good-at-snow-handling Pathfinder, and off I'd go. I have recruited in virtually every small town in the Midwest. Small towns have several things in common. One of those things is that hospital CEOs and administrators are typically products of their community or at least really understand small town living. They know the type of physician the community wants: the size, shape, color, and even gender.

In these initial interviews with a hospital CEO, I'd hear things like, "You know, Van, we're looking for someone thirty-five to forty because Dr. Jones is retiring soon, and we need a younger version to step into his shoes."

My job was to recruit doctors and to help hospital CEOs find doctors who best served their communities. Doing that was no harder than finding a tarnished penny in a forty acre pasture. The reason was simple: most qualified doctors didn't want to move to a small town. Most small towns weren't growing but dwindling. There were fewer other doctors to socialize with and fewer doctors to share calls. It was a simple case of supply and demand. Physicians, for the most part, can locate work wherever they would like, but hospitals and clinics don't have the vehicles to give their practice opportunities exposure. Nor do they have the ability to repeat the message over and over. That is the time a good recruiting company comes into the equation.

Finding a doctor who wanted to move to a small town was tough. Tougher still if the doctor was game but his spouse wasn't. The spouse didn't know people in the new town. In most small towns, everybody had grown up together and formed a tight-knit group of friends that often didn't take in outsiders. A doctor's kids didn't get integrated as quickly because all the other kids were locals. The new kid was a foreigner from back east or out west or up north.

My job was to find a physician with the right credentials, the right qualifications, the right income needs, the desire to move, and a family willing to give it a try.

Not long after I started TimeLine, I sat down with Bart Milstead, the CEO of a small hospital in west Texas. Milstead was a highly educated, forty-five-year-old straight talker from St. Louis running a hospital in Texas. His forte was working with financially troubled small town hospitals and making them profitable, and he was good at it. I sat in Milstead's office in front his large oak desk. "What kind of physician are you looking for?" I asked. "Tell me who's going to fit into your community."

"That's easy, Van, and these are not my rules. You asked me what kind of candidate is going to do well here. Number one, no female doctors. This is an all-male world around here. I'd love to have more women on staff, but our doctors are men, and they'd take to a lady doctor as well as they'd take to a case of Lyme disease. Number two, no Middle Easterners. Our town is filled with Dr. Smiths and Dr. Joneses. Our patients hunt and fish. These are people with gun racks and spittoons, and we need our doctors to fit in. Number three, no African-Americans. This isn't a personal bias. My job is to bring in a doctor who will feel welcome here, who will, in fact, be welcomed by our existing staff, and to set that doctor up for financial success. It'd be rare if an African-American made the cut. My job is also to fulfill the desires of the organization. In other words, I didn't make the rules; I just play by them."

So I took my list, returned to the office, and started doing what every recruiter does. I got on the phone and talked to doctors. This small town was looking for a gastroenterologist, so I reached for my list of gastroenterologists and started dialing. Gastroenterology was a small field, at the time probably seven to eight thousand in the entire country. I'd been through this before and I knew the process. Calling all the phone numbers, leaving messages, calling again, talking with a few, and doing all the follow-up calls would take me two months or more. I would likely make three thousand dials to find one solid candidate who would even stay on the phone long enough to hear about an opportunity. And offering a hospital client only one candidate was no guarantee of a placement.

I typically made three hundred phone calls a day. No fancy phone equipment, no auto dialer or power dialer with a database of preprogrammed phone numbers. I picked up the phone and dialed. The life of a recruiter was challenging at best. You lived in a cube: four walls, a desk, and a phone. I started at six in the morning and stopped at nine at night. I called early, sometimes waking people, because I wanted to catch doctors before they made their rounds on patients at the hospital. If no one answered, I'd leave a message.

In all that dialing, I lived for the one or two or three yes's. Most days, I'd get two hundred ninety-eight no's and a couple of yes's. I learned early that I had to embrace the word no to be any good at this business. I didn't fall in love with the word "no." I just learned how to stomach it. I knew I had to get all of the no's out of the way if I was ever going to get to a yes. I'd sit there all day banging the phones, trying different messages, different bait to get a return call. I'd leave all kinds of crazy messages. "Dr. Jones, whatever you do, do not delete this message. Don't. Just hear me out." And then I'd say what I had to say. Or, "Dr. Jones, this call is worth $300,000. Give me a shout back." Or, "Dr. Jones, I know your spouse would want you to talk to me, so give me a holler." I had all kinds of clever techniques for how to skirt gatekeepers, and I was highly successful. I never had to lie to make it happen.

When I did get a doctor to return my call, I'd introduce myself and call him by his first name. "Hey, Tim, I'm glad I caught you. I'm Van Allen, with TimeLine. I understand you might want to hear about practice opportunities."

So I started looking for a gastroenterologist willing to relocate to west Texas. The very first doctor I talked with was a guy in Rockwall, Texas, Dr. Tim Huggins. Tim was patient and mildly interested—interested enough to let me finish my pitch. I learned he was a very accomplished college quarterback and baseball player for a college in St. Louis. He had a big personality, and he was articulate and health conscious. He loved to hunt and fish. He told me about his boat, a 20-foot

Harbercraft, he'd just purchased and how he got up early on the weekends and cruised nearby Lake Rockwall to cast a line.

Several calls later, Dr. Tim Huggins and his fiancée, Ann, decided they were interested enough in the opportunity in this small community in west Texas to go for a visit. Ann was from Fort Worth, not forty minutes from the small town where this particular opportunity was located. A move would get her closer to her family, and Tim wanted to make her happy.

The first rule of recruiting was to meet the candidate in person before you put him in front of a client. On the day of the meeting, Tim and I agreed to meet at the Four Seasons Hotel in Irving, Texas. I arrived a few minutes early, and a man approached. It was Tim; I knew it. He walked up and shook my hand. He was strong and fit and handsome, the image of a GQ cover.

And he was African-American.

Tim took a seat, and I excused myself to make a call. I dialed Bart Milstead at the Weatherford hospital. "Bart, he is on his way. This is the biggest home run candidate I've ever presented a client. He's great-looking. He's qualified. He's everything you've ever wanted in a doctor."

"You're excited," Milstead said. "I can hear it in your voice."

"His fiancé and her family are from Fort Worth. She wants to move closer."

"We've been looking for a gastroenterologist for four years."

"He's well trained. Board certified."

"So you said."

"No disciplinary actions or professional misconduct. High patient satisfaction scores."

"He sounds perfect."

"He'll be there in a couple of hours."

I sold and I pumped up the enthusiasm as high as I could

get it, and I delivered the news. "Here's the thing. He doesn't look like the rest of you guys, the doctors on staff there in town."

"What do you mean?"

"He's African-American."

Milstead took a breath. "Van, we talked about this. The interview is a waste of time."

"Hold on. You have to do the interview. This guy is a must-meet. I know what you're looking for, and I know what you need. This guy is it."

"This isn't good."

"Here's the promise I'll make you. If after fifteen minutes, if you haven't fallen in love with him as I did, I'll pay for the entire interview— travel, lodging, meals, whatever it costs."

"I'm not going to regret this, am I?"

Tim and I ate a quick breakfast, and he drove to his interview and arrived at the hospital early. I returned to the office and sat in my cube, nervously awaiting some feedback. If the meeting went badly, I could lose a hospital client and dampen my relationship with Dr. Huggins. Not to mention the potential for a lawsuit if Tim felt he was being discriminated against.

Tim walked into the CEO's office and introduced himself to the executive assistant, Linn, and the interview was off to the races. These meetings are between the CEO and the doctor. I'm not invited. I knew exactly how long the meeting should take. When I figured the meeting had ended, I called Bart Milstead. He didn't pick up, and it rang and rang. Finally Linn picked up.

"Hi, Linn. This is Van. So?" I said.

"He's still in there with Bart."

"What did you think of him?"

"That is absolutely the most beautiful man I've ever seen, and he is such a perfect gentleman."

"What do you think Bart will think of him?"

"I don't know, but I don't know how you can't like him."

An hour later I got Bart Milstead on the phone. "So, am I paying for the interview?"

"This one's all mine. You sent me a rock star."

Milstead saw what I saw. He saw a human being. He didn't see color. He didn't see a member of a race or a category of person. He saw the real person. He knew he'd found the right person for the job. Milstead knew what he wanted. I knew what he needed. And color had nothing to do with it. Fast forward ten years. Dr. Huggins is still there.

I believed in Dr. Tim Huggins. Dr. Huggins believed in Dr. Huggins, and in the end, Milstead believed in Dr. Huggins and so did this small west Texas town.

As a result of that placement, this hospital developed into a steady client and provided us with countless searches which resulted in serious income for both myself and the company I was working for.

When you believe enough, it's contagious. If you want to sell something nobody wants, you need to believe. This story has another point: that the numbers can work in your favor. That's what kept me at my desk making over three hundred calls a day. I knew from experience it took three hundred calls to find one doctor interested enough to interview for the position. One in three hundred is a winner. Each time I picked up the phone, I wasn't afraid. I was excited because I knew if I could get one yes in the next three hundred calls, I was right on schedule to place a candidate. If I got two yes's, or three or four, I was way ahead of the game.

What Set Us Apart

The retained physician recruiting industry is dominated by a few giant recruiting firms. Merritt Hawkins, my former employer, was one of the biggest and one of best. In order to compete, I tried something different, something nobody had ever tried in the industry. I planned to take a one time retainer and then five months of professional fees at $2,000 a month and offer a money-back guarantee. If I didn't fill the search, I would refund the $10,000 in professional fees.

That one bold idea launched me into the big league. TimeLine Recruiting offered a money-back guarantee at a time when it was unheard of. Two months before I left Merritt Hawkins, I spoke with Joe Hawkins and outlined the same idea. He didn't like it. The downside was too expensive and the upside uncertain. The idea was wonderful if you filled searches and a disaster if you didn't, which often happened. When I started TimeLine, I needed a hook, a way in the door, and a money-back guarantee was my hook. At industry meetings and conferences, I met colleagues who told me I'd fail. Many of the industry experts said this concept would not work.

Once I put the guarantee in place, selling a hospital administrator or CEO on the benefits of using TimeLine Recruiting was easy. Well, kind of! I'd sit down with a hospital CEO and I'd say, "Let me ask you a question. Picture a large car lot. All the cars look alike, and then you spot a real bargain. You test drive the car, negotiate a price, and pay for the car. The salesperson says they offer a special service. They wash, wax, and buff the car and personally deliver a shiny new car to your home the following day. You go home and wait. The following day, no car. A week goes by, no car. You call, and the salesperson says they're getting to it. Tomorrow for sure. Six weeks go by, no car. Here's my question. At what point, Mr. CEO, do you get angry?"

The answer is always the same: the next day. The day the car was supposed to be delivered. "That's right," I'd say. "A promise is a promise. What's more painful is you've paid in advance. You've spent the money and have nothing to show for it. What I'm describing to you is Merritt Hawkins, Cejka, or any of the big retained recruiting firms that take your funds with no guarantee. At TimeLine, we tell you we're going to deliver the car, and if we break that promise, you get your money back."

TimeLine Recruiting came with a money-back guarantee. If a guarantee sounded like good business sense, I'd ask the clients to call their current recruiting firms and ask for the same promise. The established firms wouldn't do it, and here's the reason. They didn't have to as long as clients continued writing checks without getting results. The Timeline way was a bulletproof offer, and what hospital CEO could say no?

Why Doctor Searches Fail

Three things caused most recruiting searches to fail. First, I couldn't get clients to return my calls. Second, clients didn't follow up on a timely basis with candidates who fit the parameters and didn't act with a sense of urgency. And third, some clients didn't pay their bills on time.

First, returning calls sounds like a no-brainer. Think again. Finding the right doctor for the right position meant working through a pile of details, details and information I sometimes needed from the client. If that client didn't return my calls, I couldn't move forward with the search. Once again the sense of urgency was critical to success in placing a candidate.

Second, many clients failed to follow up with the candidate or candidate information I put in front of them. I might find a candidate who fit the client's parameters—specialty, education, job history—and one who might even consider moving to a wintry small town in northern Wisconsin, but the client failed to pick up the phone and connect with the candidate. Immediate follow up was critical because doctors weren't on the market. Typically, doctors didn't need the hospital; the hospital needed doctors.

If a hospital recruiting executive or CEO showed genuine interest by following up with a candidate within forty-eight hours or sooner, he created a special connection. That connection generated real interest from the doctor. Physicians do not want to go where they are not wanted. My job was to force an immediate relationship between the organization and the physician. Many times the candidate was a perfect fit for the hospital but on paper didn't have all of the qualifications the opportunity was seeking. My job was to open the funnel up a bit so hospitals would consider a wider array of candidates, making the possibility of filling the search more likely.

Remember, clients paid me professional fees of $2,000 each month for five months. In other words, there was a strong financial incentive for the hospital to fill the search as quickly as possible. I therefore encouraged clients to work closely with me, to be proactive about the candidate search. To avoid needless delays, I recommended the hospital have its physician employment contract drawn up in advance and doesn't wait until we got a candidate interested only to spend three months with the hospital's attorneys hammering out the details of an employment agreement.

Third, some clients didn't pay their bills on time, and I couldn't afford to continue a search if the client didn't pay me on time. In the early days, positive cash flow was critical to staying in business.

If I could induce a client to do all three things, my odds of filling the search were very good. And here's the catch to the money-back guarantee. Fail to do any of these three things, and the money-back guarantee was off the table. Don't return my calls or follow up with a candidate or pay the bills on time per the agreement between Timeline and the opportunity, and all bets were off. I kept working the search, but in the event I didn't fill it, I wouldn't refund the money.

Before I signed a contract, I sat down with each CEO and made sure we had an understanding. I guaranteed to fill the search, and they committed to do these three things. I made sure we took the excuses off the table early. No "I was away on business," or "I was on vacation." Most CEOs focused on the money-back guarantee and didn't realize or didn't care that in agreeing to my terms, these executives had inadvertently made TimeLine Recruiting a priority they couldn't afford to ignore.

Making the Strategy Work

The money-back guarantee strategy evolved. In the early years, I got burned several times because I offered the guarantee without any commitment from the hospital. I expected, naively, that everybody would play fair. If I offered a guarantee but my clients failed to follow up with my candidates or if they did a half-assed job of following up, I wouldn't be able to fill the position, and I was dooming my own search.

So I learned. I gave back some money, and the next contract I signed I got the client to promise to follow up. Then I had a few small hospitals put me at the bottom of the list on payday. A week late turned into a month and two months and so on. They eventually paid. It just wasn't when they said they would, and I had to scramble to pay staff, buy mailing lists and postage, and keep the lights on.

So I learned. The next contract I signed, I got the client to promise to pay me on time. I took some blows, but I learned. Ultimately, the money-back guarantee was the strategy that put TimeLine on the recruiting map and enabled me to get in front of any hospital CEO in the country. It gave me the weapons and the nerve to call any hospital or physicians' group, no matter how big, no matter how prestigious, and brazenly make my pitch. It was also the vehicle that enabled us to go head-to-head with the five-hundred-pound gorillas in the marketplace.

I'd estimate that 65 percent of my clients breeched the contract. They couldn't or didn't live up to any one of those three little terms. Once that happened, the policy was to send a nice letter informing the hospital staff they had breeched the agreement. The letter was polite but firm. TimeLine would keep working the search, but the money-back guarantee was off the table.

Even if they did meet all the requirements, I didn't fill every search. Consequently, I sent back a lot of money. There was a downside to the strategy, but the upside was that I got more business than I thought possible, and I filled dozens of searches effectively and efficiently. Moreover, I was able build a business and a business culture that focused on ethical and responsible business practices. And we focused on results. TimeLine was grounded in integrity, in doing what we said we would do, and we expected our clients to do the same. I created a business model that was profitable without taking advantage of individual clients, the board of directors, or the hospital and clinic system as a whole. I believed and put into practice a model of shared risk whose goal was a genuine win-win outcome.

Early Results

In our first year, TimeLine was awarded approximately twenty-five search contracts and earned revenue of $180,000. Based on the guarantee, I had to refund the professional fees for three of the searches. That was $10,000 apiece or $30,000. Writing the checks was painful. The remarkable thing was that almost every time I refunded money, a client immediately gave me more business. I was in the physician recruiting business, I was not filling the search, and clients gave me more business. Clients loved us when we filled searches, and they loved us when we didn't.

In truth, clients were dumbfounded each time I sent them a refund check. Whenever I did, I made a call and spoke with the CEO or recruiting director. I said I felt horrible about not filling the search. On the same call, I pointed out the positives. They could report to the board of directors they didn't squander $10,000 on a recruiting company that didn't produce results. They were prudent about recruiting expenses. They negotiated an agreement that protected the hospital. Because I made the CEOs or recruiting directors look good, they were willing to give me another shot. When I refunded the professional fees, I viewed it as an opportunity to sell. I wasn't down or morose; I was upbeat, and I didn't burn any bridges. In most every case, I was able to recoup the loss by making good on the next search.

Leading with a Negative

No business strategy is perfect, and mine wasn't even close. Leading your sales pitch with the money-back guarantee was tantamount to leading with a negative. I had to be careful how I framed the guarantee. In truth, clients didn't want the money back. They wanted to hire a doctor. That $10,000 refund was a drop in the bucket compared to the money they lost each day and each month because they didn't have a doctor on staff performing pricey medical services. The guarantee was a tool to get me in the door. Once inside, I was quick to promote benefits of the guarantee other than money, which included motivated recruiting staff, management oversight, and good old-fashioned pride.

First, our recruiters spent all day on the phone calling doctors trying to find a candidate who met the requirements. Recruiters were paid a base salary and a large commission when they filled a search. If they didn't fill the search, they didn t get the bonus. This simple bonus system made our recruiters keenly aware of exactly how many days until our five-month search contract expired. Let a search contract expire unfilled, and the opportunity for a recruiter bonus went bye-bye forever.

Second, inherent in the guarantee was management oversight. The guarantee forced managers, including me, to oversee every search because I couldn't afford to refund the professional fees on an ongoing basis.

And third, refunding the money meant accepting defeat. It meant admitting I couldn't do the job, that my zealous spiel during the initial meeting with the CEO was nothing but sales hype. Refunding the money meant swallowing my pride. An additional incentive, although not one I shared with clients, was that without the professional fees, I couldn't make it on other client revenues alone. In addition to the monthly retainer fees, TimeLine charged clients for ongoing costs, primarily direct mail expenses and advertising. We charged actual costs plus handling plus a small profit. The additional revenue helped, but without the monthly professional fees, we couldn't keep the doors open.

The guarantee got me in the door. Once inside, I quickly shifted gears and talked about the downstream benefits of the guarantee, those benefits that made most sense to the client.

Selling Your Strengths

From the very beginning, we sold our strengths. We sold the money-back guarantee. We sold my experience and history in the retained recruiting industry. We sold the idea that we were a boutique recruiting company. We offered clients individual attention. We were not like the giants in our industry, those uncaring Goliath companies where your search got lost in the shuffle of a thousand other searches. We were hands on. This was a pitch that not only resonated with smaller hospitals and institutions but also got the interest of larger hospitals that had experienced problems with the larger agencies. We sold honesty and a conviction in the truth. It was an easy sell because we believed. Belief is the habit of placing trust in yourself and in others. As a business principle, it works. Bart Milstead believed in me. I believed in Dr. Tim Huggins. Dr. Huggins believed in himself. Together we proved that even against the odds, believing is contagious.

THREE

● ● ○ ● ● ● ● ● ●

Cinnamon Toothpicks

*Simplicity is the most difficult thing to
secure in this world; it is the last limit of experience
and the last effort of genius.*

—*George Sand*

Any good business can be simplified to making a great
product and telling people about it. Customers and clients long
for simplicity. Why, then, do many business leaders, product
designers, and sales professionals confuse the complexity of
function with the simplicity of design and presentation? To my
way of thinking, creating a good business is so simple a nine
year old could do it. When I was nine, I did just that.

I came from a poor background, and my two brothers and I
were always trying to come up with ideas to make money. I was the
oldest, and when I was in the fourth grade, I looked around and
identified an untapped market: kids in my school loved cinnamon-
coated toothpicks. Half the boys in school, it seemed, had one or
more of the spicy-flavored toothpicks sticking out of the side of
their mouths throughout the day. At the time, you could buy the
toothpicks at a nearby 7-Eleven, five toothpicks for a nickel. The
only problem was that they just weren't hot enough.

Cinnamon can be mild or hot, depending on how much of the oil or powder or syrup gets soaked into the food or, in this case, the toothpick. The kids in my school loved their cinnamon toothpicks so hot they burned their mouths. The hotter the better, yet the local convenience store didn't sell the really hot toothpicks. So I got the idea to make my own. I asked my mom to buy some cinnamon syrup and a couple of boxes of plain toothpicks. My plan was to make the toothpicks hotter by a wider margin than we could buy in any store. I dipped the wooden toothpicks in the syrup and let them soak until they were good and hot. Some batches I soaked for a full week. My super-hots I soaked for two weeks. I wrapped them in aluminum foil to preserve the heat. At times, I'd forget that I had handled the cinnamon soaked toothpicks and rub my eyes. Don't do that.

When the toothpicks were ready, I let them dry and took a small batch to school and gave one to a friend, Brian Benoit. He put it in his mouth, and his eyes lit up. His eyes may have actually teared from the sting of the cinnamon on his lips and tongue. I handed out more free toothpicks, and the kids loved them because they were so hot. It was a challenge to see who could keep the toothpicks in their mouths the longest. Then some joker got the idea to put two and three and four toothpicks in his mouth and see how long he could take them.

The toothpicks were a hit. At the end of the day, I raced home and began a big, new batch of my super-hot cinnamon toothpicks. I wrapped them in tin foil in packs of five and carried the packs to school. I sold them for ten cents a pack. I became the "go-to cinnamon toothpick guy." I'd enter school each morning with my pockets full of the aluminum foil packs, and they'd be gone by noon. That first day I sold twenty of the packs at ten cents apiece for a whopping profit of $2.00, a small fortune at the time.

At nine, I learned to identify a need. I learned to fill that need. And I learned that any good business can be simplified to two things: making a great product and telling people about it.

A Father's Simple Lessons

Many of the lessons I now use in business I learned from my father. Dad was born and raised in Philadelphia. When he completed high school, he went off to a prestigious vocational school where he learned structural design and drafting. He was a hellion growing up and routinely got into trouble. He was the son of a bridge painter, and he had two siblings named Dan and Dutch.

After Dad completed his vocational training, he took a job in an oil refinery in Port Arthur, Texas. Soon he met Carolyn Cormier, my mother, a French-speaking Cajun and a Louisiana native. The two married, and after all three boys were born in Texas—Barry, Beau, and me—we moved several times. First to Los Angeles and later Palmyra, New Jersey; and finally back to Lake Charles, Louisiana.

Like most fathers, mine was bigger than life. For years, he drank too much, and then one day, for reasons I didn't fully understand, both Dad and Mom abruptly gave up drinking and smoking. He made decisions and then acted. That's the way Dad was. Just like that. At about the same time, our family began attending church. Mother had been a devout Catholic for much of her life, but until that time, Dad wasn't religious at all.

Dad was an all-or-nothing kind of guy. No in between. No shades of gray. One day he drank. One day he didn't. One day he cared nothing about the church. The next he was driven to serve.

We joined a Pentecostal church, one of those places of worship filled with people dancing in the aisle, speaking in tongues, and laying on hands. My mother and father loved it. They jumped in with both feet. Dad did everything from mow the grass to teach Sunday school. Our family was the first at church to unlock the doors and the last to leave. For years, our entire family was at the church every night for meetings, teachings, and sermons or just helping out with church maintenance.

At about this time, Dad decided we boys weren't getting enough physical education at school. To whip us into shape, he made us get up before school and run six miles. Every day. We did nine laps around the block, and Dad stood on the front porch counting the laps and timing each lap with his stopwatch. If we didn't run the six miles in our target time, we had to run another six when Dad got home from work. There were many days we ran twelve miles. After the six-mile run, we lifted weights in the front room for an hour, and after that, we gathered in the family room, where Dad read aloud from the Bible.

As Dad read, Mom was in the kitchen cooking breakfast. She was a great cook, and breakfast could be anything from French toast, pancakes, and cornbread mush to scrapple, grits, oatmeal, and biscuits. Dad loved his scrapple. This routine of running, exercise, and Bible study lasted for years and ended only when I graduated from high school.

Throughout these years my brothers and I were close. We were close for a lot of reasons but primarily because it was us against all the other kids in school. The other kids made fun of us because Dad made us do laps every day and because we didn't cuss, smoke, drink, dance, or go to movies. We didn't participate in any activity, it seemed, that Dad didn't think up himself or that wasn't related to church. We ran and lifted weights and read from the Bible and went to church. We stood out from the other children thanks to Dad's unorthodox child-rearing approach, and at the same time, my brothers and I felt unique and special and loved.

Our town had a church revival nearly every week, and the Allen family was always there sitting as close to the front as we could get. Sometimes the revivals went on for days or weeks, and I treasured the preachers for their energy and spirit. Some of the preachers were so good they could move a crowd up and down the emotional scale with little effort. People would laugh, cry, and shout all in the span of a single sentence. Even the bad preachers were a thrill to watch. Most often the revivals took place under a tent with rows upon rows of folded metal chairs and glaring lights dangling from the wooden poles that held up the tent. When there wasn't a revival in town, we'd load up the van and travel out of town until we found one.

The family I describe sounds fanatical, but in truth, I grew up in a nurturing environment. I knew my role in the family. I knew what was expected of me, and I tried my best to meet those expectations. My job was to run my laps, lift weights, go to school, and learn the Word of God. In addition, Dad gave us boys lots of chores around the house. The chores had a dual purpose: to keep us occupied so we wouldn't fight and to allow us to contribute to the family in a tangible way. We weeded the garden, washed cars, rake leaves, mowed grass, or did any other random chore Dad could think of and, in doing so, earned our place in what I see now as a close and loving family.

We were also a poor family. The most my dad earned when I was growing up was $28,000 a year. Our house at 3012 Center Street, Lake Charles, was all of nine hundred square feet. A boxy little thing that, to a child, felt both inviting and sturdy as a castle. How we squeezed a family of five into nine hundred square feet I'll never know, but we did and enjoyed the experience.

All this is to say that Dad taught me a set of values—cohesion, communication, tradition, and time spent together—that have stayed with me all these years, values that I eventually implemented in my own business. Cohesion, for example, is the feeling of being loved, of belonging to a family or group, and what better place to emphasize a sense of belonging than at work? A company can foster the best parts of family by implementing processes that have the simple goal of making people feel wanted.

A Blueprint for Change

When I graduated from high school in Lake Charles, Louisiana, I spent my first year at McNeese State University. This campus was literally three blocks from the house I grew up in if I jumped three chain-link fences. During my second semester of college and during that summer, I worked at Boys Village, where I lived with fifteen troubled kids who were basically either wards of the state or had gotten in trouble with the law and were given Boys Village as an option to rehab themselves. I always had the bug to work with kids, but this was at a whole different level.

After I left Boys Village, I went to Evangel College in Springfield, Missouri, which is the mecca for the Assemblies of God denomination. After I had been there one year, my youngest brother, Beau, decided he wanted to go to school with me, but Dad didn't want us that far away from home. So we decided to attend Southwestern Assemblies of God College. After I completed my degree, I took a youth director position in Fort Worth, Texas, specifically Watauga, Texas, where I worked for Pastor Von Lombard.

Before I accepted, I wanted one concession. As a future youth director, my biggest concern was that kids wouldn't open up to me. I felt part of the reason was that parents attended all youth meetings, and naturally most kids kept any dialogue on a cursory level because Mom and Dad were listening. I approached the church leaders and said I'd accept the job on one condition: parents were not allowed at the youth meetings. I said I would need parents to participate in many upcoming activities, but as far as developing these children by learning what was in their hearts and minds, I needed this one concession. I couldn't have parents at youth events nudging their kids or swatting them in the back of the head for speaking up.

The church elders agreed and allowed me to create what I called the Change Agent Program. I sat down with ten kids, those I felt were true difference-makers, leaders, and influencers, and I told them about my idea. The idea was this: each of the ten difference-makers would build a team of two or three other children. The leader's job was to create positive changes in those two or three children, to have a clear constructive impact, and at the same time to recruit three or four more kids from their junior high or high school until each team consisted of ten kids. And of course their main responsibility was to replicate another leader so that person could break off and build a small group of his own.

The results of the Change Agent Program were spectacular. The easiest outcome to measure was the growth of the youth program. The original youth group of about thirty kids grew to two hundred and fifty in less than a year. The less quantifiable outcomes were that the difference-makers matured and took on greater leadership responsibilities at an early age. Those members they recruited to the team who showed signs of leadership were promoted and began recruiting their own teams. The success of this program in all its forms stuck with me for many years. When I started TimeLine Recruiting, the Change Agent Program served as the model for building my own team—I hired my key staff and let them recruit their own teams.

Hiring the Team

A few short months after starting TimeLine, I had a handful of physician searches to fill and not a single employee to help me. I had no sales staff to help bring on new clients and no support staff to perform all the other functions required to run a successful recruiting company. My challenge was to hire quality staff as quickly as possible. My first hire was Mike Wills, a former sheriff in Waco, Texas. Mike lived in Columbia, and he liked it there. He didn't know anything about recruiting, but I convinced him to come on board and said I'd teach him everything he needed to know.

With Mike Wills as my first recruiter on board, I asked my brother, Beau Allen, to come work for me as salesman. Beau was still living in Nashville when I recruited him. Back in 1990, I had moved to Nashville and tried my hand at the starving musician thing and convinced Beau to join me there. We put our act together, a country music duo, and we had a lot of fun but little true success. I was a solid musician, guitarist, and vocalist. I even did some respectable songwriting. I gave myself three years. If I didn't make it in that time, I'd give it up. After three years, I packed up and moved to Dallas, Texas, where my parents and my other brother, Barry, and his family had moved several years earlier.

Beau had stayed in Nashville, and by the time I started TimeLine, he was ready for something new. As I had with Mike, I told Beau I believed in the business and I believed in him. Beau moved to Columbia. By night, he sang and played guitar at the local bars and clubs. By day, he marketed TimeLine Recruiting to hospitals and clinics. Beau did all of my marketing. He was very instrumental in the early stages of helping create the brand of TimeLine.

For the next several months, Beau and I spent a couple of weeks a month driving across Missouri, Kansas, and Nebraska meeting with hospital CEOs. At first, Beau just listened, and I talked. To keep us both afloat, we split the commissions when we won a search contract.

Three months later, in August, I hired Nora Hunter as a recruiter. She showed early signs of great leadership abilities, and she also proved she could place physicians. At the time, Nora worked for another company in the building where I had rented a small office. Each day she saw Beau, Mike, and me in a frenzy of activity, excited about each new contract or whenever we located a doctor interested enough to interview with the hospital. One day Nora stopped me in the hallway and asked what we did that was so much fun. I told her a little about the business, and she said if it was that much fun, then she wanted in. Nora was a quick study and became an exceptional recruiter. In less than two months, I put her in charge of Mike, and she and Beau became my two key people.

As I began hiring staff, I was still working for Tenet, acting as a mediator between Tenet and several key physicians. My role was to assist Tenet Health in unraveling the agreements physicians had signed with the organization. I was also responsible for negotiating the lease agreements as most of the physicians owned the buildings they practiced medicine in. I was the guy in the middle, and both sides hated me. Tenet wanted to get out of its old physician contracts as cheaply as possible and wanted me to be a ruthless negotiator. The doctors, some of whom I had hired and had since become friends with, saw me as a turncoat, an evil representative of management willing to play hard ball to shred their employment agreements.

My commitment to Tenet was that I would work at the hospital in the mornings and have my afternoons free. There I was, Tenet's hatchet man in the mornings and a nurturing one-on-one trainer for Mike, Beau, and Nora in the afternoons. I actually received many threats from employees I had to terminate. I was simply the messenger. The decisions were not mine. This was a stressful time, so to alleviate as much stress as possible, I focused on building my company. Specifically, I put my energies into creating a great product and telling people about it. Nora and Mike were my physician recruiters. These were the people responsible for locating doctors and convincing them to consider a career change. This, in effect, was my product. Beau and I were the sales team. We were responsible for telling hospital administrators and key recruiting executives what we did, how we did it, and why we could meet hospitals' needs more effectively and inexpensively than our competition. Our small team of four people had big ambitions and very clear goals. Each member of the team knew what was expected, and each had the fundamental skills to meet those expectations. If anyone became overwhelmed, if anyone made the job too complicated, if anyone lost focus, I stepped in and reminded everyone to keep it simple. Our objective at that point was to make a great product and tell people about it. Ultimately it was to win. I believed if we did all the things I taught my staff to do, we would win. That we could do.

The Genesis of Company Values

Like a family, every company follows a set of values, standards, and beliefs that drive company strategy and employee actions. In many companies, this set of values is covert and not explicitly communicated to employees. Even if it is communicated in the form of a mission statement or vision statement, these formal statements often read as if they were crafted by public relations firms and brand experts or, worse, by attorneys who want to mitigate risk by saying as little of substance as possible. Many companies pay lip service to the values as described in mission and vision statements while the real business and corporate culture is left to grow and evolve by the frontline, hands-on staff.

I wanted TimeLine to be different. I wanted to make a conscious effort to promote company values and standards that I believed in. Our mission was to build a great product To have high ethical standards. To treat our clients, physicians, and employees with the utmost respect. To care for and support our company as we would a family.

Even in those early days with just three employees, I wanted TimeLine Recruiting to be an expression of the best that family could offer. I wanted the leadership to express a positive mental attitude, to show awareness and monitor employees, and to exhibit socially positive behaviors. I wanted employees to have daily routines, spend time together, communicate, and praise each other, develop supportive relationships, and laugh. There were times that's all we could do. I wanted TimeLine to be the best. This statement was short. It was simple. It was direct, and I meant it. I believed TimeLine could mature and reach its potential only when our staff and employees reached their potential. We did just that.

Nora and Mike worked well together filling searches. Nora hired several more recruiters, and by the end of the year, we had four full-time recruiters. At the end of our first full year in business, 2001, we earned approximately $180,000 in revenue. In 2002 our revenue jumped to $300,000, and by 2003 we topped $520,000. The numbers started small and grew exponentially, and to me they were staggering. I had never seen or realized that kind of money in my life, and in some ways, it went to my head. In gaining such success so early in the process, I'd lost sight of my own business mantra: keep it simple.

The Worst Business Decision I Ever Made

Simple was boring. These weren't words I spoke aloud but in hindsight were what I was thinking. The company was growing. We had a plan, and I wanted more. Some of the challenges I faced in those early days were a consequence of not having a line of credit. I started with a check for $15,000 from Julie, my girlfriend, and I had blown through the money in days it seemed, setting up my office, bringing on staff, and traveling for business. For the first four years of TimeLine's existence, the only investment capital I had access to consisted solely of the cash the company generated on its own. I was a new company with tenuous prospects. No banker in her right mind would give me a loan. In the beginning, we operated a bare bones business.

I wanted cash flow, and I wanted to grow as quickly as possible. There was a third issue nagging at me: I simply wasn't content with one office. I had this burning desire, which I still find a little puzzling even today, to open a grand office in Dallas. Maybe part of me wanted to return to Dallas to be close to my folks. Opening a Dallas office was the perfect excuse to go home. If I could establish a presence in Dallas, what I thought of as my southern office, Dallas could handle the southern states and the Columbia office the northern. I also believed that Dallas would give us far more national exposure than we would ever receive from our lone office in little Columbia, Missouri.

The solution to all my woes was to be so eager to expand that I brought on a partner, the worst business decision I ever made. I called a former colleague, Mike, and we talked about the idea of a partnership. I had trained Mike in the recruiting business years earlier when we were both working at Merritt Hawkins & Associates. Mike had always been an all-around great guy and a top producer.

We were good friends, and we stayed in close contact over the years. Fortunately, when I left Merritt, I didn't leave for another recruiting company. I left to manage medical clinics, so I left on good terms, retaining my relationships with all my Merritt Hawkins colleagues.

That all changed when I opened TimeLine Recruiting. Merritt Hawkins & Associates and TimeLine Recruiting were now competitors, and I had effectively distanced myself from everybody at Merritt Hawkins, with the exception of Mike.

Years earlier, Mike used to tease me, saying that if I ever wanted a business partner, he'd be the first to quit Merritt Hawkins and join me. I didn't take him seriously. Who wanted to leave the best recruiting firm in the industry to work for a small start-up firm? Nonetheless, Mike and I spoke often over several weeks, and I finally asked him to join me as a partner in mid-2002. Our agreement was simple: Mike ran the Dallas office, and I ran the Columbia office. We set up a plan where Mike became a 25 percent partner the first year and a 50 percent partner thereafter. I agreed to underwrite the Dallas operation until Mike had the cash flow to support the office fully.

The plan was straightforward, but instead of a boost to the overall business, the arrangement quickly became an anchor I couldn't get loose from. First, opening the Dallas office was poorly timed. The Columbia office was doing exceptionally well but generated limited extra cash beyond what we needed for ongoing operations. Every dollar I put into Dallas would have been better spent reinvesting in an already successful operation in Columbia. I couldn't invest in both offices at the same time, and it seemed we were constantly juggling our finances to keep the Dallas office afloat. Second, Mike should not have been my choice for the job. He was a great producer, not a manager of that type of operation at this juncture in his life. Third, I wasn't involved with the start up as much as I should have been.

In many ways, I felt paralyzed by the arrangement and unable to react. I couldn't be in two places at once but desperately needed to be. A part of my management approach was to be in the office, to be present, walk the floor, talk with staff, pat people on the back, and cheer when we landed a new search contract or a recruiter talked to a physician interested in our opportunity. Recognizing these small successes was critical to staying positive in an industry where the staff had to wade through a lot of no's to get one yes. In the early years, I was part boss, part manager, and part cheerleader, and all of those parts had to be present to be effective. Yet I couldn't be in two places at once.

The Columbia office was bustling with activity while the Dallas office was struggling with hiring staff, landing search contracts, and filling those searches, and there seemed to be little I could do about it. Each month I poured more money into the Dallas office, and each month my relationship with Mike became more strained.

I wanted Mike and the Dallas office to be successful. Immediately, we divided the country into territories, and I gave Mike all of our southern clients. The Dallas office opened with a handful of established clients. He had two objectives: hire recruiters to fill the searches and hire marketing staff to add to his search inventory.

Both proved difficult. New staff did not buy into the message—build a quality product and tell people about it— and periodically I traveled to Dallas and preached the gospel according to TimeLine. I'd get the staff motivated, revved up, and ready to conquer the world. I'd leave Dallas thinking I'd made an impression, thinking the situation would improve. It didn't.

Two weeks later, the message had gotten watered down. The Dallas staff became gloomy, and employee motivation plummeted. Or worse, people quit. It seemed as though I'd have to set up camp in Dallas because nothing I did or said had a lasting effect.

A part of the reason the Dallas office struggled was that Mike spent his energies on strategy, market size and trends, budgets, employee discipline, and a long list of management basics. What was missing was focus. Customers buy a simple product with a singular value proposition. The Dallas staff did not understand that this business could be simplified to two things: making a great product and telling people about it. In my eagerness to expand, I failed to ensure that the Dallas office was staffed with those who shared and could execute my vision. Ironically, Mike and I have mended fences and have discussed at length the mishaps during our relationship and Dallas experience. Mike has gone on to do great things, and no doubt, we both learned from that experience.

FOUR

● ● ● ● ● ● ● ● ●

Don't Throw Them off the Bus

All forms of self-defeating behavior are unseen and unconscious, which is why their existence is denied.

—Vernon Howard

No business leader wants to be a tyrant. No leader strives to be a dictator. Yet some measure of organizational coordination and control is required of any growing company. Organizational control in this sense means taking a systematic approach to managing processes and people. So what do you do when someone in your organization challenges your authority by being insubordinate, by ignoring policy, or by jeopardizing your product quality? My suggestion is to give him options.

In 1985, I was living in Dallas, Texas. I was twenty-one, a student, and married. Between us we didn't have a dime. I was studying theology, and my wife was studying music. We were two idealists suddenly faced with the fact that we needed money to eat.

So what did I do? I did what you would have done if you didn't have any skills and you were in college and lived in Texas. I marched down to the bus barn and asked for a job driving a bus. The bus barn was a filthy place crowded with dusty yellow school buses. I shouted, "Anybody here?" and an old guy appeared from behind a bay of shelving stacked high with rusting metal parts. The guy had hunched shoulders and a cigarette stuck between his lips. The cigarette waggled when he spoke.

"How can I help ya?"

I told him I was looking for a job, and he asked why I wanted to drive a school bus.

"I need money."

"That's it?"

"I'm married."

"That ain't a reason."

"I like the schedule. I pick the kids up in the morning, go to class, come back at three, and drop the kids back home."

He pulled the cigarette from his mouth and dropped it on the floor, stepped on it, and mashed the butt into the concrete. "Look, I have one route open. Here's the thing. Most of my buses have a monitor, an adult that kind of corrals the kids while you drive. Only this route doesn't have a monitor." He paused and looked at me. "About a week ago, an angry mother jumped on the bus and stabbed the driver. The driver is still in the hospital. It was a big, ugly scene. The driver was pregnant, and she lost her baby. I just wanted you to know, that's all. It's a dangerous route."

I thought about it for less than a second. "It sounds perfect."

My first day, I made three quick and effortless stops. On the way to my fourth, I looked in the mirror and saw a trumpet case flying through the air. The case was big and heavy, and it hit a kid in the back of the head, and the kid started crying. I stopped the bus, stalked to the back of the bus, and yelled at the kids. "Who threw the case?" Nobody said a thing. "We're not moving until someone fesses up. We'll stay here all day, miss school, whatever it takes until somebody tells me who threw the trumpet case." Minutes later, a kid about mid-bus points to a big kid in the back seat, a freckle-faced, two-hundred-twenty-pound monster of a kid.

I look at the boy. "What's your name?"

"Dexter."

"Dexter, did you throw that case?"

"What if I did?"

"Follow me."

"I'm not going anywhere."

"No, Dexter. You're going to follow me," and I turned and marched forward with Dexter right behind me down the aisle past fifty big-eyed kids. When we reached the front of the bus, I opened the door. We were six miles from the school.

"Dexter," I said, "I'm going to let you make a decision. You can get off my bus and never come back. Or you can sit on this step for the rest of the school year. I don't care, either way. You make the call."

"I'm not sitting on this step."

"Then go on," and I pointed out the door.

All fifty kids were waiting to see what Dexter would do.

"If I get off this bus," Dexter said, "that means my mom's going to have to drive me to school every day. I can't do that."

"Then that's a problem. If I were you, I'd sit on this step and get used to it."

"I walk off this bus, and my dad will give me a beating."

"So take a seat."

"Yeah, okay, I'll just sit here." And he sat.

The lesson is that I was able to get Dexter to do something nobody else had ever been able to. I had controlled the biggest, most unruly kid on the bus by giving him options. At an early age, I learned the way to change behavior is to give people options. What would have happened if I had just said, "Get off the bus"? There would have been a fight. It would have been a disaster, and I would have gotten fired. What would have happened if I'd simply said, "Sit down on this step"? He would have been defiant and probably walked back to his seat and sat down. And I wouldn't have lasted.

How do you stand up to employees destroying your company? You don't throw them out. You throw them some options. You don't throw them off the bus. You throw them a choice that preserves their dignity. And then you have control.

Give Employees Options

Have you ever had someone in your organization who destroyed morale and intimidated other employees? Or people who merely refused to follow company policy? I've had plenty. One of the policies I implemented early on was a simple dress code. I wanted staff to look good when they arrived at the office because I believed, and still believe, that if you looked good, you felt good and employees who felt good performed better.

Columbia, Missouri, is a small, relaxed town, and many employees didn't buy into my professional dress code. Others were young or had little corporate business experience and didn't know what to wear without explicitly being told. My rules were straightforward. Men wore a pressed white shirt. You couldn't press the shirt at home; I didn't allow that You had to have it professionally pressed. Two, you wore a suit or business slacks and a sports coat. Three, you wore a tie. Four, you wore socks. You'd think everybody knew to wear socks, but I had an employee, a rodeo kid, Clay, who didn't believe in socks, he said. He complied with all the other rules, but no socks. No matter what I said, Clay would show up twice a week without socks, and in a way, I felt my authority was being tested by those bare ankles.

Clay had worked at TimeLine for about a month, and I'd talked to him about the dress code maybe five times. At first, I did it indirectly, more or less making a little joke of it. I'd walk by his cubicle and say, "Hey, Clay. Can I give you a couple of bucks so you can buy some socks?" Or I'd say, "Clay, remind me to bring some socks from the house and give them to you as a gift." He never got it, and I finally invited him into my office. When he arrived, I said, "Clay, here's the deal. You can wear socks, or you can find another place to work. If your conviction is so strong about those socks that you'd give up a good job, a job you are good at, then I'll respect your decision. I like you, but the dress code is strictly enforced."

"I've never worn socks."

"I never wore suits before I got into business."

Clay and I talked for the next ten minutes about the job, his outside interests, his family, and a couple of his long-term goals. We talked about everything, it seemed, but socks. Then he paused and said, "Okay, sure. I'll wear socks."

I let Clay know what his options were and what my standards were. I let him talk about his feelings and his options, and I let him make his own decision. That's what I did with Dexter on the bus. And that's what I did every time I needed to redirect an employee into new behaviors. If you want to change behavior, give some options. Inform about standards and let people talk it out and make their own decisions. In proceeding this way, they will never feel coerced or oppressed. On the contrary, they feel respected and will respect the decision they make themselves. That's how you keep good employees and change behavior without throwing people off the bus. Clay stayed with the company for three years and was a successful recruiter.

Keep an Eye on the Cash Flow

By early 2002, TimeLine was a whirlwind of activity. Amid the hustle in the Columbia and Dallas offices, cash flow was a constant problem. We spent money on hiring and training, yet employee turnover remained high, and we never kept people long enough to maintain a full staff. The Dallas office required a constant infusion of cash, and to make matters worse, several of our clients delayed payment for reasons that had nothing to do with us. By September, I stopped cashing my paychecks because there wasn't enough money in the bank.

About this time, we promoted four employees to vice-president, which required even more cash for the increase in salaries. I believed this was nonetheless a smart move in planning, organizing, and controlling the growth of the company. I believed the Columbia office could improve profitability with a better, more hands-on management team in place. The cash flow and management issues were stressful, and that stress made me do strange things. One week I was Mr. Nice Guy, and the following I was a picky micro-manager.

In October, I had an appointment with my banker, Tim Littikin, to discuss what he liked to refer to as our "cash flow crisis." The books showed a profit, but collecting the cash was a chore, and thus our dollars outstanding continued to rise. Tim was concerned that our line of credit wouldn't cover any shortfall or, worse, that without adequate cash flow the company might collapse and default on our loans. Tim used my own strategy on me and gave me a couple of options, but in this case I had to do both. First, I had to be more consistent and conscientious in our budgeting and spending. Second, we needed to boost revenue by closing more sales. Not easy tasks. Our payroll continued to grow, yet my key staff were still relatively green and not good enough to prospect and close sales on their own.

We'd had some successes and had recently landed several doctor search contracts with Quorum Health Group, a large hospital chain headquartered in Tennessee. The Quorum account was a huge feather in our cap but wouldn't produce results for months.

My anxiety over the company's financial standing escalated. The Dallas office continued to be a drain, and I found myself angry at my decision to expand and bring on a partner. Mike didn't have any collateral in the deal and, therefore, didn't feel the pain as acutely as I did. I think it's fair to say that nobody felt the pressure as I did. My home, business, and even relationships were highly leveraged.

One of the mistakes I made was in not sharing my concerns with the people around me. I didn't tell my wife, Julie, about the lack of cash flow, and I rarely addressed the issue with Mike. I held it all in and didn't talk to anyone because I reasoned no one could fix the problem but me.

My solution was to work. I arrived at the office at 5 AM and sat at my desk and worried about the office, about the staff, about what Julie must think of my getting up at four each morning and trudging off to work. I sat in my big leather chair and made lists and worried over each item. Before I knew it, I'd wasted several hours worrying. By the time my staff arrived, I was brimming with anxiety, and I sometimes blew up at staff or shouted at vendors. Other times, I just sat in my office, paralyzed by indecision.

As a respite to all the worrying, in November I took the staff on a trip to Las Vegas to attend a recruiting conference. I hoped the trip would be fun and strengthen the bonds within our management team. I also planned to meet with several potential clients. Each evening, we gathered for a fabulous dinner and were often joined by prospects and existing clients. My sales and recruiting staff made some great contacts, and for perhaps the first time in my career, an industry conference produced tangible results.

When I returned to the office, I was charged with new ideas, and I quickly implemented new, more stringent recruiter requirements on key production metrics. What I learned from watching my team at the conference was that my recruiting staff was not as assertive about contacting doctors as they could be. And thus I instituted new goals for phone time, search contracts, and the number of interviews a recruiter needed to schedule each day, week, and month. I did the same for the sales team, and the new standards produced results almost immediately. The number of new search contracts went up, and the number of searches filled climbed right along with it.

Each time I implemented a new standard, I tried to inject a little levity. Change can be difficult, and I understood. I didn't do things "by that book." I changed policies and standards frequently trying to find the right mix of structure and individual autonomy, and I recognized that my approach could unnerve some employees. I also learned that try as I might to stay focused on key metrics I still managed to send mixed messages to my leadership staff. I wasn't clear enough with my message, and I therefore tried to improve as a leader by improving the way I communicated. In the end, I believe my management team respected me more for my heart and passion than for any newfangled management technique I dreamed up, though the techniques and standards did in fact help.

About the time I was implementing tougher work standards, I also believed I needed some outside help getting TimeLine's brand out in front of our potential clients. In November 2002, I engaged a large public relations firm out of Boston. Hiring the PR firm was a timely move. My management team and I had the operational pieces in place, and we now needed a broader, more strategic marketing message. The PR firm and their marketing ideas were expensive—around $10,000 a month in consulting fees alone—and I nervously put a lot of trust in the idea that the marketing campaign would ultimately pay huge dividends.

No matter what strategies I put in place, the Dallas office still struggled with low morale, not enough seasoned staff, and the wrong people in positions of responsibility. Late in the year, Mike had to terminate his vice-president of business development. The woman was a solid sales person but had difficulty making the transition from personal sales to management. The result was the loss of countless sales employees and thousands of dollars spent training new hires trying to get the sales machine back on track.

In the Columbia office, I had maintained low employee turnover, and those who did leave left for personal reasons. For example, I lost an employee, Mike Kinder, who was abruptly called to the Army Reserve. Kinder was a budding star and his loss would be felt, but I quickly replaced him with a woman who picked up where he had left off.

Mike began spending more hands-on time with the staff, and this sort of commitment was just the action I was looking for. Mike's strong suit was personal production, but getting folks motivated and doing things the right way was more difficult. Despite setbacks, Mike grew his staff to about forty, which translated into a larger payroll, not necessarily more sales. In addition, the Dallas staff recognized me as the creator of the organization and therefore undermined Mike's directives in subtle ways.

I think part of Mike's frustration stemmed from the fact that he wasn't enjoying the same degree of success I was and he took it personally. Mike realized he was a burden. I had misjudged his ability to deal with criticism and take direction. In late 2002, I considered for the first time terminating our relationship.

A New Selling Dynamic

Revenue in December was lower than forecast and not the way I wanted to close the year. Late in the month, I had a lengthy training session with our sales team. My philosophy was that we needed to kiss a lot of frogs. If we kissed enough frogs, we would eventually land a prince. Unfortunately, that philosophy wasn't working. We had an astronomically high travel bill. To change our outcomes, I required the sales team to do a better job of qualifying each prospect on the phone before setting up a face-to-face interview, and I implemented new guidelines on how we were going to accomplish this.

Qualifying prospects made for a much more difficult sale. It was easy to call a hospital, speak to the executive assistant to the CEO, and set an appointment. It was a whole lot tougher to speak with the CEO before you visited and make sure the CEO was genuinely interested in hiring TimeLine to find doctors. My sales staff hated the new qualifying requirements. I told them to hang in there. I was the first to admit I wasn't sure the qualifying requirements would work, but I insisted we keep trying until we found an approach that did.

My challenge as a business leader was to build a professional sales team out of employees with little or no professional sales training or experience. Part of being a professional was identifying solutions. Any one of my team could spot a problem, but when creating solutions for clients, they were lost. My sales team was made up of presenters—people comfortable standing in front of a room and giving a canned presentation. They spoke well but didn't think. There was little give and take in a typical client or prospect meeting, and what little there was they didn't capitalize on because they didn't know how.

True sales professionals, on the other hand, were hungry for objections and probing questions from a client. Without those objections, a client had no real involvement or interest in our service. I needed to find a way to make my staff love objections, to make them better at finding solutions. At about this time, I was working with the PR firm, and solutions must have been on my mind because the PR consultants and I came up with a new company slogan: "TimeLine Recruiting—Recruiting solutions for recruiting issues."

Mike and I agreed the sales staff needed additional training, so we got together and revamped our entire selling process. Initially, I wasn't excited about the time the training would demand of me. Then I saw how excited Mike got. He was enthusiastic and more keyed up than I'd seen him in months. My office had historically outperformed Mike's, and I didn't feel the need to overhaul the sales training in Columbia as much as redirect it. Dallas, on the other hand, needed an entirely new sales approach to get things turned around. If the Dallas sales force could close as many sales as the Columbia office, we'd be in great shape.

In the past several months, I'd unknowingly lowered my expectations for both my sales and recruiting teams. My thinking was akin to "Bad was better than worse." As we approached the new year, I readjusted my thinking. I aimed higher, and I was determined to improve our profitability. I cracked the whip in the Columbia office and took a hard look at our recruiting team and especially at employees with low production numbers. In a few rare cases, Nora and I agreed to fire unproductive staff. I also asked Nora to begin a training program with all her recruiters every day and continuing for the next three months, accompanied by direct reporting back to me on the outcomes of each training and what specific exercises were expected of the staff.

All of the effort paid off for both the sales and recruiting teams. Almost immediately I got calls from sales staff out on the road who told me how well the new qualifying and selling process worked. We had landed several search contracts and had more genuine opportunities in the selling pipeline. We closed 2002 with approximately $2.8 million in revenue and a profit margin so small it's not worth mentioning. The following year, I projected we would double our revenue.

The work we did in the last several months of the year paid off. What I learned is not to lower standards in tough times but to raise them. Set clear expectations, give staff the training and tools they need, and expect that the new higher goals and targets can and will be achieved.

I learned it was critical that our sales force meet with the decision makers, the CEO or executive with authority to sign a contract, on that very first meeting. I learned that managing a sales team was not about sitting back in the office and barking orders but just the opposite. Both my vice-president of sales for the Columbia office, Beau, and I learned we needed to spend more time out in the field and less in the office. We learned that our sales team needed and wanted daily accountability, and though it was a relentless job, this kind of senior management commitment and attention to detail paid huge dividends.

Know When to Quit

I had huge hopes for the new year, yet a series of small setbacks continued to plague the operation. Each month the Dallas office had higher expenses and less revenue, and I felt there was nothing I could do. Mike and I were partners, and the Dallas office was his to run. In early 2003, Mike made a number of key hires to help support both his sales and recruiting teams. I tried to get excited, but employee turnover was so widespread that I wasn't convinced we could retain the people we needed to get things on track.

Good leaders are innovative, and they execute. Some leaders are idea people, but few can calculate the ramifications of implementing the idea, make adjustments accordingly, and then execute. Average leaders get stuck in the "what if" game or become mired in irrelevant details and never fully translate the idea into a working process or tangible actions. Even fewer leaders can get employees to buy into the idea. The Dallas staff failed to execute and did not buy into Mike's ideas. He had the biggest office in the place, but on most other levels, he was more manager than leader. Every new idea developed at TimeLine seemed to me as if it were mine. The strategies required to execute were mine.

By the middle of March, my attitude had plummeted. The Dallas office had poor revenues, an ongoing net operating loss, employee problems, and high turnover. Few of our ideas for improvements had gotten off the drawing board. Instead of looking at boosting revenue and making more sales, Mike focused on cutting expenses, a no-win game in my opinion, and I had pretty much reached the end of my rope with the Dallas office.

Mike was an awesome person, but I had not made a wise choice for a partner. Perhaps the outcome would have been different if he had paid for a piece of ownership. The lesson here was that true partners share the risk, the heartache, and all the hard work required to get a poor performing organization turned around.

The Dallas office was in a downhill spiral and took more and more cash to prop it up. My solution was to invest additional cash in outside businesses I believed would provide the income I needed to keep Dallas afloat and at the same time take care of my family should anything happen to TimeLine. If this sounds like a textbook example of reverse logic—saving your own business by investing elsewhere—in hindsight it was. Yet at the time it seemed not only logical but also mildly insightful. While Mike's office was running a loss of $50,000 a month, my office was a cash machine generating $150,000 in operating profits. Each time I put extra effort into training, selling strategies, better customer service programs, or employee relations policies, good things happened. At times, running the Columbia office felt easy, almost too easy, and that meant I needed a challenge. My challenge was to spearhead several new business ventures.

At the same time, and without realizing it, Mike and I had stopped talking to each other. By then Mike was a full 50/50 partner, and ending the partnership was not simple. I wanted a straightforward and painless divorce, but that didn't seem possible. I began to explore all my options, and I suspected Mike was doing the same.

In March 2003, I called him and explained my concerns: the Dallas office was going down fast, and I wanted to restructure our relationship and responsibilities before we hit bottom. To complicate matters, the company owed me a bunch of money, and our line of credit was collateralized by my personal assets. We had outstanding debt—bank loans, personal loans, unpaid invoices, and unpaid taxes—totaling approximately $775,000.

I offered a couple of options. Option A: Mike would take over payments on half the debt along with restructuring his office to cover his own expenses. If he chose this option, I suggested he and I not take a salary until the debts were paid in full, which would take about a year. Option B: I would take over responsibility for the total debt and retain 100 percent of TimeLine Recruiting. Mike could keep the Dallas office as a separate entity with a new name and own his new company outright.

Mike was put off by my offer but didn't respond directly. After he received my follow-up letter, however, which included a detailed breakdown of our debt, things got nasty. Then they got worse. We argued for several weeks, and I finally told him it was best that we not speak to each other. The following weekend I was sick as a dog. I hadn't been sick in years, and the strain had settled inside my body and refused to leave. I felt compelled to write down my thoughts, believing some day I could look back on these days and rationally evaluate exactly where I went astray.

"I feel I'm staring professional death in the eyes. I don't want to let my family or staff down, yet at the same time, my decision making is based on principles—honesty, integrity, and fairness—and those principles and the decisions I make will lead where they lead. I've set emotions aside as best I can. At the end of the day, fighting to retain TimeLine may be the worst decision I ever made. However, at the moment, it feels like the right thing to do."

The attorneys took over, and for the next six weeks, Mike and I let the lawyers haggle over who would stay, who would go, and who got saddled with all that debt. Three weeks later, I sent Mike a final offer to sever our relationship without a court battle. If he refused, I was prepared to proceed with a petition to dissolve the company and start a new company. I had some ideas that I believed would revolutionize the industry—ideas Mike laughed at—and I was convinced the new company would be more successful than the old. I'd had enough with business partners and vowed never to have another.

On April 1, 2003, Mike accepted my offer. The biggest financial drain in the company's short tenure was now plugged, and the company could begin to heal. In our dissolution agreement, I granted Mike and his Dallas operation the use of the TimeLine Recruiting name with the stipulation that he transition away from the name within a year. I felt allowing him to use the TimeLine name would give his new venture enough visibility to help him get off the ground. Ironically, Mike didn't believe the TimeLine brand held much sway in the health care community and quickly created his own name.

When the legal wrangling was over, I thought that was the end of it. It wasn't. My name was still on the Dallas office's ten-year lease. Our agreement stipulated that Mike would try to renegotiate with the landlord to remove my name from the lease. Nothing obliged the landlord to agree, but for whatever reason, he did just that. If he hadn't and Mike's business failed and he subsequently filed for bankruptcy, which he did, I would have been on the hook for hundreds of thousands of dollars in unpaid lease payments.

By the middle of May, some six weeks after Mike accepted my offer, the dust had settled, and I was able to reflect on the split. Dissolving our partnership was the best business decision I ever made, albeit a correction of the worst business decision I ever made.

The lesson here is that partners must see eye-to-eye on key elements of the business and what measures are most important to the business, the partnership, and the partners. To me, each office must stand on its own, must contribute operating profits, and make the company stronger in some tangible way whether in marketing, branding, sales, operational excellence, product development, use of technology, or in some other way. If those measures aren't reached or, worse, if the partners never agree on which measures are important or critical to the partnership, the endeavor will run into trouble. The question isn't who caused it, how the trouble came about, or why it happened, but when.

FIVE

● ● ● ● ● ● ● ● ●

Don't Forget to Tie Your Shoelaces

Failure is success if we learn from it.
—Malcolm Forbes

Success in business is like a balloon, and it takes only one little pin to pop it. Minor oversights or poor decisions by business owners and executives can plummet a business into bankruptcy, and any executive who doesn't understand just how fragile his business is doesn't fully understand his business. As a leader, you must know everything that's going on within the organization because what you don't know makes you vulnerable. Make a habit of trusting others to take care of nagging details, to make decisions in the best interest of the organization, and to care about your business as much as you do, and you are in for a rude awakening. I know because I did just that. I abdicated small, seemingly routine tasks to my staff without following up, and my company nearly came tumbling down.

In December 2003, I got a chance to participate in my favorite pastime—College Division I football. What's better than going to the stadium to watch College Division I football?

Seeing your team make it to a postseason bowl game! The bowl games are typically in sunny locations like San Diego, San Antonio, and Miami—warm weather spots northerners like me crave. My team, the University of Missouri Tigers, finally made it to the Independence Bowl, and I got a chance to head south and watch.

The magical spot for the game was Shreveport, Louisiana. Okay, it wasn't San Diego, but it was warm, and it was my team and my home state. I'd waited for just such a moment for five long years. At the time, my daughter, Reagan, was three and my wife, Julie, and I decided to take her along to the game.

We boarded the plane with Reagan dressed in a cute little three-year-old cheerleader outfit, and she was so excited she screamed for a solid hour and a half. Screams of joy, we thought, but it turned out she had a massive earache that subsided only once we landed. We drove to the hotel, and our arrival was like coming home, everyone dressed in black and gold Mizzou colors. The three of us couldn't have been more excited about the upcoming game. We found our room and unpacked. Then I got a phone call on my cell phone from my long-time accountant, Dale Young. "We need to talk," Dale said. "We've got a problem."

"Nothing could dampen my spirits," I said. "Fire away.'

"On Monday morning, three days from now, the IRS is shutting you down."

"What does that mean?"

"Think big chains and hefty padlocks on the doors."

"You have my attention."

"According to my contact at the IRS, you've got an outstanding tax bill of $200,000. They've sent you letter after letter. You ignored the letters, and they have no recourse, so they claim, but to lock your doors."

"What if I didn't get the letters?"

"That's history. If you want to keep the doors open, write them a check, and it'll all goes away."

"For $200,000?"

"Just like that."

"I don't have that much cash."

"Then that's a problem."

"Can you buy me some time?"

"This is the Internal Revenue Service. They don't sell time."

"Call whomever you spoke to. Ask for more time."

No response.

"Please," I said. "Make the call. A week. A few days, even."

Nothing.

"Make the call," I shouted, "and phone me back in five minutes."

I hung up and looked around at Julie and at Reagan bouncing on the bed. I couldn't speak. I walked to the door, opened it, and walked down the hall. I took the elevator to the lobby and stared dumbly at the crowd of football fans smiling and pushing and shouting at each other. I walked outside to the pool where it was cold and free of people. The area was an expanse of cement with unused wooden lounge chairs folded into themselves. I unfolded one of the chairs and sat.

I took my cell phone from my pocket and placed it on my lap and stared at it. And waited. Five minutes turned into an hour, an hour into two. I thought about my predicament. I didn't have $200,000 because I had spent all my cash in hiring staff, business travel, direct mail campaigns, and on a handful of spectacularly bad investments. Every penny the business took in was used to keep us afloat. I had charged this trip on my credit card.

I had built a thriving recruiting company with impressive gross revenues but zero cash flow, and now the IRS was threatening to shut me down. I was thirty-nine years old, and I felt seventy. I thought about how I'd gotten here, and I began to cry.

The truth was I had failed to pay my payroll taxes, and I knew it. I wanted to blame the whole thing on my bookkeeper, a nice guy, possibly too nice to deliver bad news and therefore who had simply gunny-sacked bad news hoping it might vanish if not openly addressed. For my part, I had turned a blind eye to our bookkeeping practices, late government filings, and slippery accounting practices despite how important they were. I was focused on turning things around in our Dallas office on growing our client base, and on ways to get our clients to pay in a timely manner. Clients owed us a huge pile of money, and we had a long list of search contracts about to be filled. Filling a search meant a large bonus which led to even greater revenues. On paper, the business was a money machine. In practice, I didn't have enough extra cash to cover my own salary. Each time we hit a cash crunch, I demanded the bookkeeping staff find a short-term fix, which often resulted in shuffling funds from one account to another until we received a big payment from a client and righted all the accounts.

Any self-respecting business leader knows the importance of paying your payroll taxes—federal income tax, social security tax, Medicare tax, and state income tax withholdings. My bookkeeper, along with our accountant, had set up a separate bank account to hold the tax funds until they were due and we forwarded them to the IRS. At times, this fund was quite large. I had no intention of touching the funds, yet at some point, I did and used the money to cover critical expenses. The decision to use the money was mine. It was a bad decision, and I knew it.

Eventually the IRS sent us a tax bill. I had glanced at one or more of the bills or at least heard about them. And I ignored them. Each month the late fees and penalties compounded, and each month I experienced a sort of slow financial death.

I did nothing and trusted my bookkeeping staff to come up with a solution. If no solution was found, then at a minimum I expected them to worry right along with me.

Now all the worry and inaction had caught up with me. I hadn't meant to violate the tax laws, but I had. I hadn't meant to do any harm to anyone—investors, employees, or family—but I had. I was never so frightened in my life.

I picked up my phone and punched in Dale's number. He didn't answer. I called again. And again. I heard footsteps and recognized Julie's gait as she marched up behind me. She was angry and stood next to my lounge chair, staring down at me. She said she'd been looking for me for hours, calling my phone.

"I couldn't pick up."

"Why not?"

"I was crying."

"What's going on?"

"I couldn't stop crying."

She reached down and pushed my legs aside and sat on the lounge chair. "What are you doing out here? I want to know, and don't tell me nothing."

I looked past her and watched a maintenance man push a plastic garbage container with wheels on it across the deck and through a metal gate.

"Where in the hell have you been?"

So I told her the whole ugly story.

My phone buzzed. It was Dale. "Tell me you got a week."

He said he had good news and bad. The good news was that I had until Wednesday to raise the money. The bad news was that Wednesday was five days away. He said if I didn't come up with the money, there would likely be additional penalties. I could go to jail. I hung up, and Julie and I talked about ways to raise $200,000. She called her mother, who agreed to loan us $60,000. I called Dale and told him $60,000 was the best I could do. Dale wasn't optimistic but said he'd talk with his contact and get back with me early next week.

I don't remember a thing about the game or the rest of the weekend. What I remember is Dale showing up at my office Wednesday morning and asking for a check for $60,000 He took the check and left and returned several hours later. The IRS accepted the $60,000 as a down payment if I agreed to pay $5,000 a month for the next two years or so. If I missed a payment, the deal was off and they locked my doors until the balance was paid in full.

What I learned from that experience was that success is as fragile as a giant balloon, and it takes only one pin prick to destroy it. One misstep or oversight of a key process and months or years of hard work could vanish in a whoosh of air. If you think you can give a piece of your business to someone else, if you're not good at accounting and you think you can hire a bookkeeper, manager, or consultant to take care of the numbers for you, if you think there's anything you can afford not to be good at, think again. Your success is your responsibility and no one else's.

My bookkeeper did mention the letters from the IRS but did so in a way that I didn't pay attention. He didn't convey a sense of urgency or genuine worry. He didn't convey consequences. What he conveyed was meaningless numbers, and as far as payroll and accounting were concerned, I wasn't a numbers guy. I was a sales guy. I was a strategy guy. I was the guy with the big plan, and the details I often left to others.

I learned I couldn't delegate the numbers. I couldn't afford not to be a numbers guy. And of course, today I'm a numbers guy.

The Saga of Nurse Exchange

One of the reasons I didn't have access to sufficient cash was that I had plowed over $300,000 into a startup company,

Nurse Exchange, a nurse staffing agency. For all I loved about starting, owning, and running TimeLine, Nurse Exchange was the venture I thought would take me to the promised land. I got involved with Nurse Exchange and the company's creator, Kevin, because I found his business concept irresistible. Kevin, of course, needed money.

Nurse Exchange was set up to help hospitals locate and hire short-term nursing staff. In a typical temporary nurse staffing model, the hospital paid the staffing company an hourly fee, say $50 per hour per employee. In turn, the staffing company hired nurses and paid them $30 per hour. Thus the agency's revenue stream was based on margins.

The innovative idea Kevin came up with was to automate fully the staffing process using a Web-based interface. In order to appreciate the model, you must understand how temporary hospital staffing was performed at the time. Imagine a typical hospital with five floors. The first floor is the emergency department and operating facilities. The second floor is labor and delivery. The third floor is the critical intensive care unit. The fourth and fifth floors are hospital beds and convalescent care. Each floor operates twenty-four hours a day based on three eight-hour shifts. Each floor has its own floor manager who arrives each morning and takes a look at the patient count, reviews what nurses are out due to vacations or sickness, and decides exactly what the staffing needs are for the floor for the day. Let's say the floor manager needs three nurses for the evening shift. She calls the hospital scheduler and says she needs two LPNs and one RN.

The scheduler gets on the phone and calls her PRN pool, an internal pool of nurses who routinely work for the hospital and who have volunteered to pick up extra shifts. The problem with internal resources is that, invariably, the shifts that need to be filled are the least desirable—Friday or Saturday night or Sunday morning—and because the PRN pool staff already work for the hospital on a routine basis, they know what is desirable and what isn't and often beg off on the undesirable shifts.

Once the scheduler has exhausted her PRN pool, she begins calling outside staffing agencies who, in turn, call their pool of available workers. This manual calling approach results in lots of phone messages and voice mail and lots of time spent waiting for return calls. The process is slow, and by the time a nurse responds to the agency and the agency gets back to the hospital scheduler, the schedule might have already been filled via another agency.

This process played out every day for every floor of every hospital throughout the country. It was chaotic and wasted time and effort. What Kevin created was a software package linked to digital pagers. Each of Nurse Exchange's nurses carried a pager. Today we would use cell phones and text messages but back then texting didn't exist. As soon as the scheduler got a call from the floor manager who knew the staffing needs the scheduler simply logged in to Nurse Exchange's Web site, typed his needs, and hit send. No scheduler, no agency phone calls, no wasted effort. Instantly, every nurse in our Nurse Exchange network received a message that listed the job and the hours needed. If the nurse wanted the shift, she pressed a code, and the position was filled. Nurse Exchange allowed hospitals to fill shifts in minutes rather than hours. No phone calls, no voice mail messages, no call backs, and no confusion.

I believed we could quickly grow the number of nurses in our network using a multi-level marketing approach—getting nurses to recruit other nurses and paying ten cents for every hour worked by anyone a nurse referred. In this way, Nurse Exchange would grow almost overnight, thereby creating this huge network of nurses. We built our bank of nurses using a complex multi-level marketing model that incentivized nurses to recruit nurses in their downline.

When we rolled out the new model, we held extravagant promotional events and invited hospital executives, floor managers, and nurses. We might have as many as three hundred nurses show up at an event, and we encouraged them to sign up with the Nurse Exchange network.

In hindsight, we had two flaws in our concept. First, the software was ahead of its time. We failed to communicate to hospital executives that a Web-based application was a way to save millions of dollars in time and labor costs. Where traditional staffing companies were charging hospitals $50 per hour per nurse, we were fully automated and therefore had less overhead and charged only $38, or about 30 percent less than our competition, while paying our nurses the same. So everyone was a winner. We could fill the position in a fraction of the time. Hospital executives simply couldn't let go of the old staffing paradigm. Some thought it was too good to be true. Some thought such a deep discount meant we would shortchange our nurses and wanted nothing to do with it. Others didn't understand or trust the technology.

Second, using Nurse Exchange meant reassigning or terminating current scheduling staff, and most hospital CEOs were extremely resistant to doing that. The new approach didn't require schedulers at all because the floor manager could log in and request staff as easily as the scheduler. The irony is that just a few short years later several staffing agencies built successful businesses around the same Web-based model we proposed and today are thriving.

Once Kevin and I agreed to become partners, I handed over $100,000 to pay for programmers to complete and test the software application. The second month, I dropped another $100,000. By the third month, we were supposed to have a viable product, several sales, and the company would start repaying my investment, but it didn't happen. So I handed over even more cash. What I didn't know, and Kevin didn't tell me, was that the software was a long way from being complete. In fact, he had six more versions to roll out and test and debug before we had a salable product. Consequently, instead of investing my money to build a company—to hire key people, put processes in place, advertise, and market the concept, in other words, to do all the things necessary to generate revenue—Kevin and his team of programmers were endlessly fiddling with the code.

Months into the project, when I asked where all the money went, Kevin explained that programmers weren't cheap. And he had his own salary of $120,000 a year to cover, in hindsight a fat salary for a company with zero earnings. The fourth month, I dished out another $10,000, then $20,000 and $30,000, and on it went. Six months past our "go live" date, we still didn't have a working program and no realistic date for completion. And Kevin continued asking for more money. He was smart and shrewd, and he managed to wheedle out of me as much as $50,000 at a time.

Months passed and I made more incremental investments. The money drain continued until the total hit $300,000, and I had to admit to myself the business was failing, not from design, but from poor execution. By then, Nurse Exchange was on the brink of disaster, and Kevin and I were already on the outs. Our partnership began to unravel in just over a year. Kevin was an absolutely brilliant man, a smooth professional with excellent presentation skills and poise. He was highly creative but couldn't turn ideas into tangible products or services. I was the money man, and Kevin was the quirky genius.

When I first met with Kevin, he elegantly presented spreadsheets and detailed flow charts of his ideas. He was unusually succinct and precise in his language. He offered timelines for software completion, company infrastructure, sales forecasts, and repayment of the initial capital. None of that ever happened. About the time I stopped putting money into the company, both of us hired lawyers. Two years after we began—after plowing $300,000 into software that never worked and after $60,000 in legal fees—we settled our disagreements, and I got the product. I became the proud owner of a couple of broken laptops, some obscure software code written in an obsolete language, boxes of really nice Nurse Exchange t-shirts, and some little balls they call stress relievers. Not a bad investment if you like white t-shirts.

As I learned, minor oversights and poor decisions by business owners can plummet a business into bankruptcy, and any executive who doesn't understand just how fragile his business is doesn't fully understands his business. The same applies to businesses that never get off the ground. Kevin and I made several poor decisions. We didn't fully understand our constituents—hospital CEOs who couldn't afford the bad press from firing people in exchange for technology. Today, the environment is different, but in its time, this cost-cutting approach would have come across as uncaring, as selling out. My mistake was in believing we could translate passionate ideas into action. In a sense, I was blinded by Kevin's passion, by my own passion for what I saw as a stellar product.

I learned that passion, all by itself, doesn't translate into a viable company. I learned that people have core strengths, and once we deviate from those strengths, our effectiveness wanes. Kevin's core strengths were vision and technology, not in carrying out plans or in executing ideas. Kevin had conviction. What caused me to misjudge our chances for success? My overly optimistic trust in people and ideas, based on the power of words and not actions. I trusted that an innovative idea would overshadow any technical or operational shortcomings. I trusted people and ideas without that healthy dose of skepticism common to all successful entrepreneurs. And for all that misplaced trust, I paid a big price.

Why Distractions Are Deadly

Dissolving my partnerships with Mike and Kevin wasn't the only business I needed to quit. Back in late 2002, I met Karl, a Web marketing consultant who suggested we start a multi-level marketing company, Liberty for You. Karl laid out a plan how we could sell turnkey Web sites to small business owners using a MLM model. The idea was to get business owners to buy one or more Web sites to promote their products. By offering financial incentives, we hoped business owners would refer more business owners.

Karl made a strong pitch, and I bought in for $100,000. In May 2003, we got the company up and running. When I first got involved, Karl's organization seemed legitimate. Multi-level marketing companies could be tricky accounting, ensuring that all cash is accounted for and distributed properly. A few months into the business, something didn't seem right. The cash from sales and operations didn't add up. It was difficult to get hold of Karl and his staff, and I felt uneasy about the organization. By now, I had gotten good at untangling myself from business partnerships. With Karl, I was able to recoup my investment and a small profit, and I simply walked away.

Also in May, as Liberty for You was just getting off the ground, I purchased USMO, a company that sold phone systems to businesses. The gentleman who sold me my first phone system at TimeLine, Joe Jennings, approached me and asked if I wanted to discuss a business opportunity. Joe said his employer was going out of business and we had chance to purchase the company at a cut-rate price, around $80,000. The company came with inventory and would start making money, Joe said, in short order. I said yes. Joe was my salesman, and we employed a technician to install the phone systems. So we repackaged marketing the company and renamed it to give it a more up-to-date name, USMO.

What I learned was that peddling phone systems wasn't an easy sell. At about this time, new voice-over Internet protocol (VoIP) technology, which allowed voice communications over the Internet, was on the rise, a technology Joe and I knew nothing about.

The reality was that every business had a phone system, and companies tended to ride that horse until it dropped. If Joe wasn't aggressively knocking on doors, he wouldn't sell a thing. I prodded, and Joe sold. We did about $100,000 in revenue over the next twelve months. Just after we closed the deal, I purchased a whole bunch of used equipment because I was told I needed an inventory of parts for older systems. I ended up paying $20,000 and filling three dumpster-sized containers with equipment I never used. USMO struggled along for a year, and by October, I couldn't give the business away. I know because I tried, and no one would take it. Soon thereafter, I walked in and said the party was over. I dissolved the organization. This was one more example of my getting involved in a business I knew little about. Purchasing USMO belongs on my list of the worst decisions I ever made.

Malcolm Forbes, founder of *Forbes* magazine, once said, "Failure is success if we learn from it." I wholeheartedly agree with the concept. I also agree with the implied logic, which is "Failure is simply failure if we don't learn from it," and at this point in my career, I was a slow learner.

At just about the same time I lost interest in USMO, I funded Med X, a medical billing company. Med X was created to help small- and medium-sized clinics outsource their medical billing. Services included assisting with managed care contract negotiations, medical coding of treatments, medical billing, and collections. Finally, this was a business I did know something about, though admittedly less than I thought.

In October, we went to a little town outside of Columbia, Missouri, called Mexico to sell Med X services. We planned a big presentation with a large health care organization with multiple hospitals and several clinics. Over the phone, several of the clinics liked our service offerings enough to give us a verbal commitment. Unfortunately, the presentation was a disaster, probably the worst presentation I ever delivered. I walked into a buzz saw of objections about our reimbursement philosophy, coding structure, electronic claims, patient inquiries, management reports, collection policies, and a host of other details I just wasn't prepared to address.

Nonetheless, I believed the company would be a winner. I even invited my brother Beau to join me in managing the company. We had great people at the top of the organization, or so I thought. It turned out I didn't match people and positions as well as I could have, and after months of selling with little results, the company never really got off the ground. Add one more to my list of failed business investments. Med X was a distraction that prevented me from putting my full efforts into growing my core business, TimeLine Recruiting.

As harebrained as these ventures now seem, they made sense from at least one standpoint: years earlier I had purchased a large office building in Columbia to house my TimeLine office, and I figured each new business would rent inexpensive space in the building. The cheap rent allowed my partners and me to start a business with very little capital and lower overhead, and I personally would generate cash from the rents. Putting all my business activities under one roof didn't work, of course, because the businesses didn't last. What I took from these experiences is that nothing is a sure thing. Nothing is guaranteed. And nothing is sacred. Money, no matter how hard you worked to earn it, could be squandered if you didn't fully understand your business.

Any executive who doesn't understand just how fragile his business is doesn't fully understand his business. I ignored my own advice. I made a habit of assuming others would take care of the nagging details, make decisions always in the best interest of the organization, and care about my business in the same way I did. I didn't truly understand any of these businesses, and I paid a hefty price for that lack of understanding.

SIX

●●●●●●●●●

Keeping Up, Staying Ahead

We've all heard that we have to learn from
our mistakes, but I think it's more important to learn
from successes. If you learn only from your mistakes,
you are inclined to learn only errors.
— *Norman Vincent Peale*

In 1992, a short seventeen years ago, the Soviet Union had just collapsed, Wal-Mart Stores, Inc. was too small to make the Fortune 500 list, our federal debt was a paltry $4.0 trillion, and a gigabyte of computer memory cost around $4,000. Today Walmart leads the Fortune 500 list, our federal debt has nearly tripled, and a terabyte hard drive (one thousand megabytes) costs around a hundred bucks. It's easy to forget just how fast the world is changing. Trying to keep pace can be daunting. Just when you think you're the master of something, you're probably outdated.

In 1992, I knew exactly nothing about running a business. What I knew was shoes. I was then, and still am, a big shoe fan. I love shoes so much that I am constantly buying more. I have a closet full of running shoes, golf shoes, and shoes for every occasion. I have casual shoes, custom boots, balmorals, bluchers, and brogues. I go for funky shoes, and one of my favorites is called a monk strap shoe. Monk strap shoes have a buckle and strap instead of lacing. My very favorite is a double monk strap, a shoe with two buckles.

Some time ago I was looking for another pair of monk strap shoes. I happened to be in Dallas, and I went from shoe store to shoe store and couldn't find a single pair. I finally walked into Nordstrom's and strolled to the shoe department with its enormous array of men's shoes. As I eased around all the displays, a saleswoman walked up and asked if she could help.

"I'm looking for a particular style—monk straps."

"You didn't see any on our displays?"

"No, and I've looked."

"Have you looked at other stores?"

"As a matter of fact, Dillard's, Macy's, and some of the upper-end shoe stores downtown."

"You've looked at a lot of stores."

"I have."

The woman paused here and fiddled with the collar of her blouse. "Is there any chance the shoe you're looking for is out of style?"

This was an embarrassing moment, and it caught me off guard. She was right, of course, and I knew it the moment she said it. I was so busy looking for monk straps that I had missed the obvious. Monk strap shoes had become outdated. I had become blinded by my own nostalgic tastes and preferences, so much so that I wasn't aware of new styles dominating the market. And I was the shoe guy. What I took from this humbling experience was that in today's world, just when you think you're the master of something, you're probably outdated. By the time you reach mastery, it's all over, and innovative new products have likely flooded the market.

As another more painful reminder of how quickly our ideas can become outdated, sometime after my split with Kevin and

Nurse Exchange, I took the laptops and computer code to a programming expert in Kansas City and asked him to see what I had. He said the program was brilliant, but the programming language itself was completely outmoded. It would cost me hundreds of thousands of dollars to start from scratch and convert the code from one programming language to a newer, more sophisticated language. This expert handed me one of the laptops and said what I held in my hand was akin to an old leaky boat that needed to be hauled up on shore and retired.

Kevin and I had missed our window of opportunity on many levels, and it turned out that even had we been able to produce a working program, it wouldn't have been long before we had to update our proprietary application using newer software and programming languages we knew nothing about. In other words, even had we succeeded, in a couple of years we'd have had to start all over.

One of my perpetual errors was in hanging on to false hopes. I did it with the Dallas office of TimeLine, Nurse Exchange, Liberty for You, USMO, and Med X. I was a dreamer, and dreamers have a tendency to overlook the obvious and keep their eyes on the dream.

As times got especially tough at TimeLine, I stumbled upon another dream: sell the business and take my money and run. In February 2004, I had a meeting with a competitor, the decision makers of CompHealth, a physician staffing company. They expressed an interest in buying TimeLine. The thought of paying off my debt enticed me. No more payroll. No slow paying clients. No tax problems. If I could get enough cash out of the deal, I'd sell TimeLine lock, stock, and barrel.

After several years of steady revenue growth, the revenue had leveled out. TimeLine was awarded new contracts and subsequently filled searches, yet we did it at a pace considerably slower than we used to. At the same time, I remember reevaluating the future of physician recruiting. The business had changed in subtle ways that I hadn't seen coming. Clients had higher expectations. Competitors were ruthless in cutting fees and driving down margins. Sales and commissioned employees took for granted large bonuses and became disgruntled when they didn't earn the bonus. I had serious doubts about my sales team's ability to bring in new business, and I had just as many concerns about my recruiting team's ability to fill those searches.

Without noticing, I had a truckload of problems I hadn't anticipated. Yet I was a man who wanted to run things, who wanted to be in charge, who loved the challenge of turning a poorly performing operation around, and here I was so deep in a hole that I started to think working for someone else wasn't all that bad. I'd take home my $150,000 a year and be happy with that. No worries, no concerns, just a paycheck and more time to spend with my family. At this low point in my life, if the folks at CompHealth had offered anything close to a reasonable offer, I would have taken it. They didn't, and I thank them for that. After the meeting, I regained my senses. I gathered my courage, and I took a hard look at myself.

I had been accumulating stuff for years—shoes, cars, airplanes, and houses. Julie wasn't an accumulator. Well, she accumulated different stuff. I was the guilty party because I had become lazy-minded and comfortable. I looked around and asked myself why I needed all this stuff. I began to question my own business decisions and for the first time looked at my track record of businesses outside of TimeLine. If I had to grade myself on tangible results from these businesses, I deserved an F. This kind of self-assessment is not for the faint of heart. It's painful, and if you wallow in your failures, you just might do more harm than good. I'm not a wallflower, and it wasn't long before I changed my outlook.

For months I had been distracted. I had too many balls in the air. I had too many outside influences driving my decisions and my business. Yet I had to admit I was a dreamer. I craved competition. I enjoyed business strategy and creating new processes. I loved being the boss. The key to changing my business was changing my thinking, and it was time to devote my full attention to TimeLine. First, I quit trying to do everything. Second, I put all my effort into the one aspect of my business I felt would have the biggest return: finding the right mix of sales and recruiting staff.

The Challenge of Staffing

Maintaining the right mix of employees was always a chore. We were either understaffed or overstaffed. We went through phases where we needed recruiters and therefore hired everyone we could get. Not long thereafter, our payroll would spike, and search contracts fell. We found ourselves with way too many recruiters for the business we had. At the worst of these cycles, I cut staff, and, as unpleasant as that was, I did it. Days later, it seemed, we didn't have enough people to manage all the new business our sales team had just landed, and the cycle started all over again.

The physician recruiting business is composed of two distinct functions: sales and recruiting. The sales team went out and convinced hospitals to award us a search contract, and the recruiting team located doctors and told them about the opportunity. Each team was composed of employees with radically different sets of skills. The sales team was composed of presenters and needed to master only one pitch—they talked to the prospect and introduced TimeLine Recruiting. They outlined the money-back guarantee, and they were done. Clients awarded us a search contract, or they didn't. The pitch was the same no matter the territory, no matter the size and type of hospital—veterans' administration, mental health, community, public, or teaching. The good news was that this one pitch took very little time to learn.

A recruiter, on the other hand, had to learn a long list of special skills, most of which revolved around communication. A recruiter communicated with CEOs, boards of directors, and doctors on a daily basis. A recruiter had to know each medical specialty, for example, and not just at a superficial level but the technical procedures, income, training, and certifications. A good recruiter must investigate, drill down deep enough to analyze a doctor's current needs, and compare them to the opportunity.

For instance, if a family practitioner claimed he was generating $700,000 a year, the recruiter needed to break that number into components. In doing so, he was likely to discover that $300,000 was generated from expert witness consulting or some other kind of side work that really didn't have anything to do with what the practice generated. The recruiter must be astute enough to recognize that no general practitioner could generate $700,000 in take home pay through his family practice alone and therefore must know and be willing to ask additional questions. Training a recruiter was a long and challenging process.

Recruiters needed to communicate at a high level and at the same time speak plainly enough to get to the point and ensure that doctors were sharing accurate and complete information. They had to be smart enough to talk comfortably with a range of professionals and aggressive enough at getting past the office manager or head nurse. And they had to manage several searches at once.

I could hire and train sales staff fairly quickly. Put them in the field, and the good ones would start bringing in new business almost immediately. So far so good. Only I couldn't hire recruiters to fill searches and expect them to produce for several months or longer. Recruiters had a much longer learning curve. The biggest headache to running a recruiting company was finding a sensible mix of sales and recruiting staff.

A good marketer brought in six or more search contracts a month. A good recruiter filled one or two searches per month. In my early years, when I worked a desk, I would have months where I had six or more placements in one month. And I never placed less than seventeen physicians in a year. My all-time record was twenty-two in one year. When I started recruiting doctors at Merritt Hawkins, I lived across the street from the office, and I was in my cubicle by 5:30 each morning. I left around ten at night. I worked through weekends, Saturdays, and Sundays. True, I had zero responsibility at the time, but I had a burning desire to prove myself and to be the best I could be. And I wasn't alone. A handful of others did the same.

Somewhere between my days at Merritt Hawkins and the start of TimeLine, the business environment changed, and I missed it. In a way, my thinking had become outdated. I had to stop comparing my staff to myself. I also had to stop thinking this was the 1960s or 1970s or 1980s when older workers, mostly Traditionalist and Boomers, were dedicated to the job and had a powerful, consuming work ethic.

Younger people wanted a life, not just a job. When we hired employees, I never found people as hungry for success as I was in those early years, at least not in the way I defined success. My younger staff members were far from workaholics. In fact, if there was a shortcut to any process, to any procedure, or to any technique, they would simplify the method to its essence and skip all the steps in between. This didn't mean they were any better at their jobs, only that there were fewer steps to failure, but they wanted to earn the same money.

Without my knowing it, quality of life had trumped financial goals, and I'm the first to concede there's something to that. In my view, quality of life doesn't mean you can't be aggressive in business or driven to close the deal or, ultimately, that you can't strive to be the very best you can be. There's nothing wrong with striving for the limits of your potential in your work and life.

The Value of Hard Work

The mistake I made was in searching for another Van Allen. I was aware how much money I'd generated for my previous employer, and I wanted a handful of money earners on my staff. I used to imagine finding a bunch of younger me's, workers who had a passion to produce and fill search contracts.

I was a product of a generation that placed a very high value on work. I can remember as a kid selling cinnamon toothpicks, mowing lawns, digging irrigation ditches, and rolling fiberglass in the neighbor's sweltering attic. If I wasn't working in my own yard, I was in somebody else's pulling weeds. There was always some kind of work around and people willing to pay me to do it. All that work shaped who I am. I don't think kids and young adults are wired that way anymore. I don't know if that's good or bad, but I'm thankful for what my work ethic did for me. As a kid, we didn't have Gameboys, Xboxes, or Wiis. Growing up was about hard work. When I wasn't working, I spent time with my family. When we went to a baseball game, the whole family went. When I played Little League, the whole family came out to watch.

Today, young people are more independent and at the same time feel more entitled. The thinking goes: "I went to college, I'm educated, I earned my degree, I paid my dues, and I deserve to earn a high income with lots of benefits and a corner office overlooking the golf course." These misguided youth come to a job interview expecting the benefits without all the hard work.

I want to say to job applicants, and especially recent college graduates, that a diploma certifies they have completed a course of study. That's all. Now the slate is clean. The fact that these young job applicants are brilliant, if indeed that's the case, doesn't entitle them to anything. Now is the time to blaze their own trail, to create their own future; that future takes a lot of hard work.

The Sales/Recruiter Mix

The solution to TimeLine's staffing issues, and to my own outdated way of thinking, was to stop looking for junior Van Allens and start looking for people eager to learn. My challenge was to find ways to motivate this new breed of employee, and my approach wasn't so much a matter of external motivation as creating a model where employees had exactly enough work on their desks to keep them constantly struggling to keep up. If I could find employees who enjoyed the process, who accepted and enjoyed the challenge of routine, who enjoyed being part of a team, then I believed the company's revenue and expenses would be better aligned and we would be poised for rapid growth.

After analyzing stacks of individual performance data, I discovered the right mix of sales and recruiting staff was one marketer to three recruiters. I factored into the mix a range of variables. For instance, I looked at search contract attrition. If a marketer brought in seven searches in a month, invariably two would fall off. Most often a search was cancelled by the client for various reasons, or we might cancel a search if we determined it was unfillable—if the client had failed to structure the position properly or the compensation was inadequate to attract the high caliber candidate the hospital wanted. In such cases, we diplomatically declined to do the search.

So seven searches turned into five, but hopefully those five were solid, and spread among three recruiters on a rotating basis, we could handle them in a timely fashion. In this way, I put it to the sales staff that their responsibility was to keep the recruiters busy with sufficient business. The recruiters' responsibility was to fill searches, typically one a month, in a timely manner. My new plan of attack was to limit the number of searches a recruiter was to work. That number ranged from eight to twelve at any given time. This provided the recruiter with some diversity with respect to types of specialty searches as well as different geographical locations. It wasn't so many searches that the recruiter could cherry pick or go after the low hanging fruit, but it forced them to manage their book of business. It allowed recruiters to focus on a very small number of searches, to know the requirements of each search in detail, and to learn and be able to communicate a positive image of the hospital, community, and regional attributes off the top of their heads. By working on a smaller book of business at a time, each recruiter could tell potential physician candidates about any aspect of the job: commute, median home price, cost of living, schools, crime, arts, parks, sports, and a host of quality of life issues that might interest the candidate. In other words, recruiters became intimate with the opportunity they represented.

I committed to the 1:3 salesperson to recruiter ratio even when the numbers got skewed, even when a salesperson had a bad month and sold only two searches and not seven and therefore one or more recruiters had little to do. I held my ground when the sales staff had a banner month and sold far more searches than we could expect to fill. I didn't fire employees when times were lean, and I didn't hire when we had a glut of work. I held steady and asked the sales and recruiting teams to do their part. When required, I shifted searches from one recruiter to another, or I might ask two recruiters to work as a team.

Almost immediately, the new approach paid off. I was able to stabilize expenses by not hiring waves of employees in large batches. Employee turnover dropped, and the recruiters were able to fill more searches because a smaller workload led to higher understanding of the search requirements and more confident staff when a recruiter spoke with a doctor. The strategy worked, and it took only two actions: recognizing my own outdated way of thinking and creating a plan and sticking with it. In many ways, determining your company's employee mix is old school, but for me, it was a fresh look at motivating and challenging employees whom, for some years, I wasn't sure I fully understood. By setting aside my own beliefs about hard work and success and instead finding challenges that might engage younger workers, I discovered a way to make a big impact by focusing on a relatively small element of my business.

SEVEN

● ● ● ● ● ● ● ● ●

Crayons Won't Save You

You must take personal responsibility. You cannot change the circumstances, the seasons, or the wind, but you can change yourself. That is something you have charge of.
—*Jim Rohn*

Great leaders like Nelson Mandela, Winston Churchill, and Mohandas Gandhi are known for having good judgment, for making good decisions based on wisdom and knowledge. How then do we evaluate leaders who make decisions based on little knowledge or even bad information? I would suggest that leadership is more than gathering the most current data and passing out obvious advice based on perfect information. Genuine leadership is about taking responsibility for decisions even when grossly misinformed. When I was young, I learned this lesson the hard way.

In high school, my mother got me a job working for a small plastic laminating company called Derma Graphics. The company preserved documents like diplomas by smearing the individual diploma with a special solution, covering it in plastic, and throwing it in an oven; out it came sealed for life.

My boss, Joseph, was an earnest and serious man trying to build a successful business. Each day, he got out of the office and hustled, trying to gain new companies. At one point he approached Coach Schwarez, the football coach from our local Sulphur High School. Coach Schwarez was renowned in the state of Louisiana because he held fifteen state championship titles. In addition to his coaching duties, Coach Schwarez was responsible for organizing the year-end graduation ceremony. Of particular interest to Joseph, Coach Schwarez was responsible for producing all of the diplomas for graduating seniors.

I had been on the job maybe a week when Joseph arrived at the shop one morning and told me about his meeting with Coach Schwarez. He said he might be willing to give us all the diplomas to laminate, but first he wanted to do a test run. He wanted us to take one of his personal documents and show him what we could do. Coach Schwarez's test document was a cherished photograph with Bear Bryant, the legendary college football coach for the Alabama Crimson Tide. The picture was Bear Bryant and Coach Schwarez kneeling under the goal post, taken years earlier at a coaching camp.

Joseph said the connection with Coach Schwarez could turn into one of the biggest accounts in the company's history. He handed me the photo and told me to make it look great. I was seventeen at the time, my second week on the job, and so excited I was shaking.

The laminating process couldn't be easier. I dipped the photo in a solution, covered it in a heavy plastic, baked it, and was done. We used two types of solutions to preserve documents: one solution for original photographs and another for copies. Joseph said he was heading out for lunch and for me to go ahead and laminate the photo. I asked if the photo was an original or a copy, and Joseph thought about it for a moment. He lifted the photo and looked at it closely and told me it was an original.

"Are you sure?" I asked.

"Trust me," he said and turned and left for lunch.

I dipped this priceless original photo of Coach Bryant and Coach Schwarez in the solution, and immediately the faces started to dissolve. I yanked the photo out of the solution, wiped it clean, and watched it dry.

I had used the wrong solution. Or rather, I had used the right solution, the solution for original photos, and because the image had dissolved, I knew the photo must be a copy.

Moments later, it seemed, Joseph returned. I stood there speechless. staring at the photo on the counter. I knew I was done. I'd be fired, my mother would be disappointed, and I was disappointed in myself. Joseph strolled in, and I slid the photo across the counter. The look on his face was like nothing I'd ever seen. He glanced from the photo to me and back to the photo. He stared blankly around the room. His eyes rested on the label on the bottle of solution I had used. He exhaled, and I could see that he knew what had happened.

"The photo is ruined," he said.

"Yes, it is," I said.

"I made a mistake."

"I should have tested the paper."

"You wouldn't have known."

"But I should have."

Joseph's face reddened, and his eyes went glossy. He reached for a box of crayons and pulled out a pale color and began to draw on the photograph. He scribbled for a moment and stood and looked at the photo and bent over the counter and scribbled some more. He turned the picture to me at intervals and asked what I thought. "Does it look like Bear Bryant?" he asked, and the question would have been funny given some other context, if he didn't mean it, if he wasn't hoping for a miracle or some inspired intervention to right this horrible wrong.

I don't remember what happened next. I do recall that we didn't get the contract. Derma Graphics closed its door not long after. Even at the young age of seventeen, I felt the pain and anguish of failure, both for myself and for Joseph. I was misinformed, but it was I who made the mistake. Twenty-three years later, every time I tell that story, it still hurts. I cared about Joseph, and I cared about his company. I wanted him to succeed. The lesson is that leaders care about other people's success, and leaders take responsibility for their actions, even when misinformed.

I used this lesson to build my own company, and while I got credit for all the successes, I also made sure to claim the failures. I insisted firmly and loudly that employee mistakes based on faulty information or flat-out misinformation were a matter of poor leadership and not a matter individual performance. Whenever possible, I did what Joseph failed to do. I stepped in when mistakes were made and claimed my failure. I propped up my employees and told them the mistake was mine to bear; the guilt and remorse were mine to endure. Most importantly, I asked employees to learn from my mistakes.

The Saga of Mary and Shelia

One of my mistakes was misplacing trust. Mary was one of my early hires. She was fun, always laughing, always supportive, and a home-grown girl from Columbia. Her father was a respected cardiologist in town. I hired Mary as my office manager, and immediately she helped with just about anything the business needed. She made vendor calls, worked through our information system problems, balanced our books, managed the hiring process, and resolved human resource and benefit issues. She did everything. In fact, in the early days, there wasn't any aspect of the operation Mary didn't have a hand in. She was always available, and she always had my back.

My wife, Julie, loved Mary, and we often participated in activities outside of work. When Julie and I had our daughter, Reagan, Mary was the first person we trusted to babysit. When Reagan was two or three, she and Mary regularly spent the day together on play dates. When the business was struggling financially, Mary helped me work with the bank and juggle funds to keep the company afloat. By late 2003, Mary knew every aspect of the business—our income and expenses, cash reserves, and outstanding accounts receivables.

At one point, I noticed Mary's behavior changed. She was distant and reserved. She didn't engage with me in the playful ways she had over the past several years. Some time earlier I had hired Shelia as the company accountant. She was a CPA and came highly recommended. In November 2003, Shelia approached me and wanted to talk in private. I invited her into my office, and we sat.

"Why I'm here," Shelia said, "is I know you're struggling financially. You seem stressed much of the time and distracted. I don't know how you plan to pull through this. And, well, we have a buyer that might be interested in purchasing TimeLine Recruiting."

"Who is we," I asked.

"Mary and I."

"May I ask who the buyer is?"

Shelia paused and thought for a moment; then she nervously began a convoluted explanation of her thoughts about the business. She believed TimeLine was in trouble. We had difficulty collecting money on our direct mail campaigns. She alluded to other cash flow problems. As my accountant, she told me that she was aware how close we came to not making payroll each pay period.

"Who is the buyer, Shelia?"

She finally confessed that the buyer was Mary's father, a successful pillar in the community, and he was prepared to offer $50,000, maybe a little more.

"How did he arrive at this number?" I asked.

"Well, he wasn't interested at first. To come to the table, he wanted to see the books."

"You shared my books with Mary's father without my permission?"

"I guess I did, yes."

I told Shelia I didn't have plans to sell and that I was disappointed in her, that I couldn't imagine any breach of confidentiality more unethical for an accountant than disclosing my finances.

I was disappointed in Shelia but more so in Mary, a woman I considered a long-time friend. I had, it seemed, trusted the wrong people. I decided to terminate Mary that afternoon. Terminating her was perhaps one of the most difficult decisions I had ever made. It didn't matter that she had conspired to share my private information with her father or that her loyalty was gone or that her attitude had turned sour. Nonetheless, the one thing I wanted most from my employees, even above performance and productivity, was loyalty and respect.

I had done a lot of terminations over the years, and I handled this one better than most. I simply called her into my office and before she sat, I told her she was terminated effective immediately. I would have fired Shelia as well, but I wanted to have her review the books with me before she left. I never got the chance because she resigned within a few days of our conversation.

The godsend in this whole nasty affair was that I replaced Shelia with a current employee, Nicole Hoffman. I had initially hired Nicole as part of the sales team, but on a recent business trip, she had been hurt in a car accident and was now under doctor's orders not to travel for a while. Just as Shelia was making her departure, Nicole came in to tell me she couldn't travel.

"Listen," I said, "have you ever done any bookkeeping?"

"No," she said, "But I learn fast."

Nicole wasn't a formal accountant; nonetheless she was the best accountant I ever had. I gave her the position, and her first priority was to do an immediate audit. What she found was a pile of unbilled client invoices. There were tens of thousands of dollars that simply weren't billed.

My knee-jerk reaction was that Shelia was incompetent, but she wasn't. I still believe she was setting me up to sell for pennies. I thought this was the stuff of made-for-TV movies: hiding a huge source of untapped cash, disclosing my books to a third party, and orchestrating an offer to save me by buying my company out from under me.

I believed if I was loyal to people, they would be loyal to me. If I was generous, if I treated people with kindness, if I treated people fairly and equitably, they would return the treatment in kind. I learned a quick, harsh lesson. I learned that no matter how much you love somebody, no matter how much you give somebody, it may never be returned.

Surviving a "Mutiny"

My troubles were far from over. In December, I was playing golf in a tournament at Club Porta Cima located in the Lake of the Ozarks, enjoying a short vacation with Julie and Reagan. I was out on the course when I received a call from Nora Hunter, my vice-president of recruiting. I was standing on the sixth hole with an eight iron in my hand, and I was feeling pretty good about my game. I had just parred number five.

"I'm afraid I've got some bad news," Nora said.

"Can it wait until I finish my round?"

"We've had a mutiny. Four of our best recruiters just quit." At the time, we had only thirteen recruiters, so we had effectively lost a third of our recruiting staff.

"What the hell happened?"

"They went to work for Shelia."

After Shelia quit TimeLine, she started her own physician recruiting company and managed to lure away my best staff. What I couldn't understand was why they would leave. I knew these people intimately. They earned a good base salary and large bonuses. They were like family. Over the next several holes, I tried to call each of them on their cell phones and at home. They didn't want to talk. I was angry and hurt, and there was nothing I could do.

I believed that if I created the perfect culture and the perfect environment, no one would ever leave. I was good to people. I paid well. I treated them with respect. I tried to bond with my staff, and we occasionally did things outside of the office like play golf and meet for cocktails to celebrate a great month or a new account. I created what I thought was the perfect culture, but that wasn't enough.

My golf game was shot. My attitude was low, and I finished the round only because I didn't want to let my team down. I talked with Julie, and we decided I would drive back to the office that afternoon. Julie and Reagan stayed at the lake house. I quit the tournament and climbed into my car. My first order of business was to hire and train four new recruiters.

What I took from this episode was this: create a solid business model and others will try to copy it. Given a chance, they will often steal your employees and clients. One solution to protect your company from employee raiding is to have employees sign a non-compete agreement not to compete with you within a defined geographic territory for a specific period. A non-compete agreement won't keep people from quitting, but it might make them think twice before going to work for a competitor. Also tighten your client information security. Consider implementing measures to keep client information under lock and key and restrict access to those who need to know. Don't make it easy for current employees to leave and take your clients with them.

Rebuilding TimeLine

The simultaneous defection of four of my top recruiters was nothing short of a colossal nightmare. I could always hire new recruiting staff. Hiring wasn't the problem. The problem was how to manage all the searches these four employees left behind. One recruiter may have been managing ten or more searches. That's ten different CEOs, specialties, and geographical regions, and every one of the accounts was at a different stage in the recruiting process. That left me with forty or so searches to distribute among my remaining eight recruiters, all of whom already had a full workload.

And if hiring, training, and distributing the workload wasn't hard enough, we had another problem. Hospital CEOs hated employee turnover in their recruiting agencies. They hated to lose continuity with a recruiter because the recruiter had gotten to know the hospital recruiting team—the human resources staff, recruiting contact, physicians, nurses, hospital administrators, and others. A good recruiter had developed a strong understanding of the vision and direction of the hospital. Losing a recruiter meant losing that relationship and starting from scratch with another recruiter. And hospital CEOs hated it.

Given this aversion by hospital CEOs, I had to hang on to recruiters, even those with weak skills, because a positive attitude and strong relationship were often all it took to keep a client happy. Facing a CEO and going through a long, torturous explanation why I lost their recruiter was a painful process. Nonetheless, it was something I had to do. As a leader, my responsibility was to take on the most painful chores.

I called each client and said how sorry I was about losing the recruiter assigned to the account. I assured each CEO that I was personally overseeing searches and that I would make sure we continued to generate candidate activity. I promised to do everything we could under the circumstances. And as long as these top-level executives got the call from me, they gave us the benefit of the doubt. Ignore CEOs, neglect them, or just let some routine issue languish until it blossomed into a problem and we could lose clients.

The recruiting and training process took nearly two months, but in the end, we brought on four new recruiters, redistributed the work, and got back down to business. The year 2003 was a tumultuous one filled with serious distractions. Each time I cleaned up one mess, another came rolling my way, and I vowed that 2004 would be different.

Doing Nothing Will Kill You

Positive changes don't just happen. They take creative ideas, planning, and execution. If some aspect of your business isn't working, if your clients aren't inspired to work with you, if your employees aren't motivated to close the sale, or if you as a senior executive aren't enthusiastic about stepping foot in the office, then it's time for a change because doing nothing will kill you. In the spring of 2004, I stumbled upon a strategy to get my clients excited, my staff motivated, and my own heart pumping a little faster.

I was in the office when I glanced out my door and noticed Andrew, one of my savvy sales reps, pacing in front of the fax machine. I asked what was so important he had to guard the fax machine. Andrew said he had a shot at five search contracts from a single hospital. Five search contracts were a bonanza, and Andrew could hardly contain himself. He hopped from foot to foot like a boxer and stared at the tiny off-white machine. He said the hospital recruiting coordinator was supposed to fax over the signed contracts some time ago.

"How long have you been standing here?"

"About an hour." Andrew stared at his shoes. "Maybe longer."

"How certain are you?"

"I'm sure."

A hospital typically gave us a verbal agreement over the phone and faxed the sign contracts sometime later. Later could mean anything from hours to weeks, and Andrew looked as if he was prepared to camp out until he received his fax.

"You're confident about this?"

"Yes, I am."

"Where is it?"

"The hospital? Paducah, Kentucky."

"Let's you and me fly out and pick up the contracts."

I had purchased a $1.3 million Piper Meridian two years earlier. This baby was a single engine turbo, six-liter rocket. Man, she had some get up and go. The Meridian was pressurized and had all the navigation and aviation equipment I'd ever want. The Piper Meridian was a cool plane and served several purposes. First, I loved to fly. Second, I had a new daughter and wanted to see more of her. Traveling by car or commercial airline from Columbia to anywhere was slow, and I could save weeks out of the year by flying myself from client to client. Third, my staff loved to have me pilot them around. It made them feel like kings and queens, and that was just the mental picture we needed to close a sale. And fourth, once I started hiring more staff, the Meridian was a classy tool to get the best sales people to come work for me. I told job candidates I was committed to their success, and I was willing to make it happen in a unique way. If the deal was worth it, I'd fly them to their meetings myself in my private plane. What started as an expensive toy or an excuse to see my daughter more became a great tool for motivating my staff, hiring new sales professionals, and marketing my business as a sophisticated, cutting-edge organization.

Andrew said, "Really?"

"If you're that confident."

"I am."

"All right, then. Let's go."

We flew out to a small hospital in Paducah, Kentucky and caught them off guard. Our arrival forced the decision makers to make up their minds. Sign the contract or don't. There we were, the company CEO and the salesman in our pressed suits and wide smiles. We were dedicated, and we proved it by showing up in person to pick up the contracts and answer any questions the CEO or recruiting coordinator might have. How could they say no to that kind of service? They couldn't.

Andrew and I arrived at the hospital, walked into that CEO's office, and twenty minutes later walked out with a five-search deal. Five searches were huge, and our new client was convinced we were the right firm.

After that first experience, I began to use the Meridian as a closing tool. If the deal was big enough, I'd spend several hundred dollars on aviation fuel, load up my team, and go get the business. Why wait around for two weeks staring at the fax machine when we could get face-to-face with a CEO or other decision maker in a matter of hours?

Buying planes started as a selfish activity and turned into a major advantage for me, my staff, and my company. What do most people do when they have a passion or an idea that makes sense to them but doesn't to anyone else? Absolutely nothing. What do most sales people do when a prospective client says the contract is in the mail, sitting on someone's desk, or waiting for committee approval? Nothing. What companies should fear most isn't change, competition, or the economy. The real danger is doing nothing because doing nothing can kill them.

What's the investment you didn't make because you thought it was too much money or too much time or simply too wild of an idea to implement? How many customers have slipped through your fingers? How many sales have you lost sitting around doing nothing? What can you do to prevent a client from saying no? I would encourage you to think of innovative ideas to motivate your staff, astonish your clients, and close more business. Make the investment. Implement the idea. Do something different. What do you have to lose?

What I Learned from Mark Cuban

I had recently attended a speaker symposium in Dallas. Speakers included Margaret Thatcher, George H. W. Bush, and Tony Robbins. All of them gave these wonderful twenty-minute talks intended to get the audience pumped up. My favorite speaker was Mark Cuban, owner of the Dallas Mavericks basketball team, who at the time looked like a mature twelve year old. Cuban stood behind the podium in his jeans and tee shirt and pointed high into the seats. He told us that years ago he used to come to Reunion Arena, and all he could afford was the cheapest seat, way up at the top. During the game he would sneak down to a better seat behind the bench and watch the Mavericks. And now, he said, as if a bit hard to believe, he owned the team.

Success sounds simple when you tell it this way—when you leave out all the difficult events and tough decisions and the long periods of struggle. The longer version of becoming a billionaire at thirty-seven is that Cuban had his share of setbacks. When times got especially tough at Broadcast.com and before he sold the company to Yahoo! for $5.9 billion in Yahoo! stock, he was forced to cut expenses. His company was hurting financially, and one of the many areas he cut was free pop for the employees. He stopped dispensing Coke, Pepsi, and gourmet coffees, and he cut back on little things he thought no one would notice. The cuts backfired, and immediately employee morale plummeted. The lesson Cuban shared was that taking away something as simple as a twenty-five cent pop could absolutely destroy the morale of an organization. If you're going to cut, he told the audience, cut in areas that hurt you, the business owner, and not your staff.

Cuban's advice resonated with me. I took it a step farther. When sharing the wealth, share with everyone. When cutting expenses, cut those things that affect you, the business owner, and your senior management team first and cut expenses that affect your frontline staff only as a last resort.

When I came back from the symposium in November 2004, I made several changes. I implemented a policy to buy the staff lunch on Fridays and to have everyone leave work at three o'clock. The short workday allowed people to go the lake, golf, or just spend time with their families. I also took a play from Mark Cuban and began giving away free pop, coffee, and tea. I did a host of small things I believed would build or enhance our culture. I occasionally had lunches catered for special announcements or company-wide training, or I took the entire staff out to dinner at one of Columbia's upscale restaurants. Rather than a formal dinner, I occasionally invited the staff out for drinks and to socialize at a local bar and grill. I encouraged everyone to invite family and friends.

The cocktail hours were a way of networking, a way for me to meet friends of current employees and see if they might make good sales people or recruiters. There might be sixty new faces at one of these little impromptu happy hours. I moved from table to table and talked to people. I introduced myself and asked what these new faces did for a living, if they were happy and if they loved their jobs. If the answer was no, I invited them to come visit me at the office, and I gave them a card. The social hours were more than a recruiting tool; they were a simple way to boost morale, build loyalty, and have fun at the same time. One of my favorite things in the middle of summer was to go buy boxes of ice cream sandwiches and pass them out in the middle of the afternoon. I did random things all the time. I would wheel eight cases of beer into the building in the middle of a workday. Everything was an effort to continue to build the teamwork and exciting culture which I believed encouraged production and loyalty.

Great leaders take responsibility for revenue, expenses, and profits, but they also pay attention to the less tangible aspects of running a business. My responsibility was to surround myself with people I trusted. My responsibility was to be more aware of company morale and try to prevent good employees from jumping ship to go work for a competitor. My responsibility was to pay more attention to our accounts receivables and to pay my taxes on time. My responsibility was to do the small things needed to improve our company culture because those things could make a big difference.

EIGHT

● ● ● ● ● ● ● ● ●

Out of Gas, Out of Sync

A lot of us have jobs where we need to give people structure, but that is different from controlling.
—*Keith Miller*

How can you impose structure on employees and not stifle creativity and personal drive? One way is to provide an environment where goals are clear and objectives and milestones are well defined. Equally important is understanding the power of limits and restrictions. Far more damaging than too much structure is no structure at all. On a client visit in late 2003, I found out just how exhausting the lack of formal structure could be on my staff and me. I was traveling across Minnesota in the middle of winter. It was cold and dreary, and there were large patches of snow in the bottomland next to the highway. One of my sales staff, Lisa, was with me. She was bright and energetic, and at that point in her career with TimeLine, she still needed some hand-holding.

TimeLine's clients were located all over the country, but we had a large concentration in Minnesota, Kansas, and Nebraska, as far north as North Dakota, and as far east as Ohio, big sprawling states where the space between hospitals might be two to three hours. Scheduling several appointments in a day was tough and meant lots of road time sitting in the rental car staring out the window.

One of my travel rules was that I didn't drive. I conducted the meetings, I did all the talking and introductions, and I kept us on point. I asked my staff to plan the trip, schedule the meetings, copy the maps, know where we're going, and do the driving. Lisa and I were in the middle of Minnesota. It was cold, the side windows were fogged, and there was nothing to see outside the car, even if we could. We had finished our first meeting at nine that morning and were on the road to our next about three hours away. I told Lisa I was taking a short nap.

I woke an hour later and looked outside. Nothing but snow. I looked at the gas gauge. "Is that gas gauge broken, or are we on empty?"

"We're on empty."

"Well, we probably need to stop and get some gas."

"There's no time. We're late for our next meeting and two hours away."

"We're not going to get to our meeting if we run out of fuel."

Lisa gripped the wheel, glared at the gas gauge, and hunched forward hovering over the steering wheel as if I might steal it from her. "We have to make it."

This was Minnesota. It was winter. It was blistering cold. I said, "Call the CEO. Tell him we need to reschedule."

"There's no cell phone service. I've tried."

"That's a problem. Let's not worry about the call. Let's worry about getting some gas, and then we'll deal with the meeting."

We drove and drove and finally saw a sign for a town north of Highway 2. According to the sign, the town was twelve miles away, and I honestly didn't think we'd make it. We limped into town, and it looked like a movie set from an old black and white Western with small houses, gray and weathered. Dirty snow was pushed into the gutters. The bare shrubs reminded me of tumbleweeds. What I felt was decades of neglect. Main Street was deserted. A skinny dog stood on the corner and watched us go by. Lisa and I stared at the gas gauge.

We came upon a gas station of sorts and coasted up to the pumps; we both let out a long sigh. It was an old gas station. The two pumps were slender and rounded, the paint peeling and the numbers on the display large and clunky, pre-digital. This was a place where, in its day, an attendant pumped your gas, aired up your tires, and washed your windows. Now, it was vacant. Not a soul in sight. I walked up to the window and tapped on the glass. Nobody came. I walked across the street to the post office, and inside I said to the lady, "Ma'am, I'm out of gas, and I'm at this gas station across the street. Do you know if the owner plans to open today?"

The woman had yellow hair and a wide face. "Do you have a card?"

"A card?"

"You've got to have a card."

"A credit card, you mean?"

"That won't do you any good. You can't get the pump a-going unless you've got the card."

"Do you have the card?"

She thought about it for a moment. "No."

"Do you know anybody who does?"

"There's a bar across the street. You can't miss it. Ernie, the bartender, he's got one."

I walked across the street and pulled my jacket tightly around me to ward off the cold. I waved at Lisa sitting in the car and pushed open the door to the bar. It was dark inside, almost black at 10:30 in the morning. There were a couple of men in work clothes hunched over a table on my left. I was in a suit and felt out of place. I waited for my eyes to adjust, and I took a few steps and saw another man behind the bar.

"Yes, sir," he said, "can I help you?"

"Are you Ernie?"

"Ernie's not here."

"I'm at the gas station a couple of doors down. I need gas."

"Do you have the card?"

"That's why I'm here," I said and shrugged.

"I don't have the card. These two," he said gesturing at the men at the table, "they don't have a card. Ernie, he's got the card, but he's not here."

And all I kept thinking was that I was late for my appointment. I was mad at Lisa for not filling up the tank, mad at the bartender and his two buddies for no reason at all, mad as hell at Ernie because he was the only person who could help me and was nowhere around, and mad at myself for being in this position.

"Man, I really need some help," I said. "Do you know where I can get the card?"

"Right next door is the combine shop."

So I trudge next door and entered the combine shop, a massive warehouse filled with harvester parts, tractor wheels, grain platforms, and large cutting tools with metal and plastic teeth. I walked in, and no one was around. I yelled, "Hello." This little old guy who walked out was wearing greasy overalls. He stopped a few feet away and looked me up and down.

"How ya doing? My name is Van Allen. I'm next door at the gas station."

"Let me guess. You need the card."

"I do, yes. If you could help me . . . ."

"I don't have one. I know some who do, but they're out in the fields or on their farms."

"You've got to be kidding. Would you mind explaining what this card is?"

"I can explain it, but it won't get you down the road. That gas station used to be a full-service job back I don't know when. The owner's a farmer, and he doesn't have time to sit around in town waiting on people. He created a set-up where all the farmers get a card. If you're part of the farm co-op, all you do is put your card in the machine and fill up your truck, your combine, or whatever, and every once in a while you get a bill in the mail."

"It won't take a credit card?"

"Nope."

"Without some gas, I can't leave the gas station."

"Looks like I'll be seeing you around," he said.

I walked back and talked to Lisa. I told her the story, and just as I'd finished, a farmer in an old pickup pulled up to the pump next to us. It was one of those pickups with an extra fuel tank in the bed of the truck and a long-handled pump on top. The guy who stepped down out of the truck was wearing coveralls, a jacket, gloves, and a ski mask it was so cold.

"Sir, do you have the card?" I asked.

"Yes, sir. I do."

"Can I pay you in cash for some fuel?"

"I don't see why not."

I filled up, and off we went. We drove two more hours, never once got cell service, and arrived at the hospital late. I turned to Lisa and told her not to worry about it; we would address what happened later tonight and come up with a game plan to make sure it never happened again. At that moment, I needed positive energy. I wanted her game face. I told her I would do all the talking and all she had to do was relax and take notes. We had experienced a set back, and I made a decision to laugh at the moment and lift our spirits with some levity so we would be ready to tackle our next meeting. It wasn't going to do us a bit of good for us to both walk in stressed-out and worked up over something that was completely out of our control.

I walked up to the administrative assistant and introduced ourselves and explained a short version of what had happened. I asked if the CEO was available.

"Let me see," she said.

We waited and waited and waited. The CEO finally arrived and said he had a few minutes. We walked in, and I went through the whole story. He kind of chuckled because the small town where he grew up was much the same. I went through my TimeLine Recruiting pitch, and he gave us the business on the spot.

Trust Must Be Earned

That trip to Minnesota was a hard way to learn a lesson. Up to that point, I assumed other people who were intelligent, as Lisa was, would think like me. My model of the world shifted that day from people are similar to me to people need structure. They need clear instructions and interpretations of guidelines every step of the way. This single event created a paradigm shift in my way of thinking: people are not like me.

This experience had been impossible for me to foresee because it was difficult to imagine. In a sense, I had a failure of imagination. I didn't have in my world paradigm that somebody could fail to stop and get the fuel needed to make the next appointment. Once I shifted my paradigm, once I understood that not all intelligent employees thought as I thought, that not all staff prioritized or juggled several logistical issues at once, I changed my own outlook on sales and training, and I began to run a tighter ship.

In short, I had assumed Lisa would make decisions as I would. Many times our failures are the result of attributing to our people qualities they don't possess. We want to coach them and mentor them to be as capable as we are, and we refuse to see those capabilities from any perspective but our own.

I trusted Lisa because when I interviewed her, I looked for a person who could handle the details. Marketers have so many balls in the air that they must be extremely organized and foresighted. They must think things through. They must be able to think at many different levels. During our initial job interview, Lisa said enough of the right things to convince me she wasn't someone who would overlook something as basic as filling up the gas tank before a trip.

I'm a recruiting expert. I know how to size up people. I'm constantly interviewing physicians who have to be meticulous and methodical. Yet with my own recruitment, I missed the fact that this woman couldn't think big picture. What I learned from this experience was not to trust people to be exactly like me or to be as meticulous and compulsively on-point as I was. I learned not to assume everyone was the master of the obvious.

Structure, Structure, Structure

In some respects, the card story incident was trivial. Things go wrong, mistakes are made, and clients are usually understanding. Yet coming on the heels of so many larger miscalculations like failed business ventures, unbilled receivables, losing staff, and unpaid taxes, the incident caused me to take note, and in turn, I reevaluated myself and my sales team. My sales team was mostly young twenty-somethings, men and women from the millennial generation born from the early 1980s to early 2000s, and this young cohort was most productive when given lots of freedom and latitude at work. It was hard to get them to sit down and take direction, the literature said. Managers must loosen up, assign clear goals, and let your millennial staff figure their own way of getting there. I disagreed. I believed in structure and fundamentals in any business activity. I wanted steps in the process done in a certain way and in a certain sequence because these steps and sequence had worked for me. I was a recruiter first and a manager and business owner second. I knew the hard work involved in getting a hospital to award us doctor recruiting business, and I also knew what didn't work.

Beau was in charge of the sales staff, and with his help, we rewrote all of our sales training and performance procedures. We addressed the sales process, territory, travel, compensation, management practices, support, and continuous development of our staff. We outlined the objectives and listed unambiguous and incremental steps that, if followed, would lead to predictable outcomes. We spent weeks training the staff on the expanded procedures, and in the end, far from being put off by this detailed structure, the sales team loved the procedures. If they had a question, they knew where to find an answer. They knew the rules of the game, and the challenge was how to work within those rules to win the game. If they couldn't find an answer to their question in the procedure manual, they asked a manager who talked to me about it, and we'd amend the manual.

I believe employees want structure in their lives, and I provided it. My staff didn't have to guess what time to show up to work. Work started at 7:45 AM. You could arrive earlier, but if you showed up past 7:45, there were consequences. You could leave late, but if you left before six, there were consequences. If I noticed you taking many smoke breaks throughout the day, there were consequences. If I saw you on your cell phone repeatedly, there were consequences.

This formal structure also applied to attire. When we visited clients, the men wore a white shirt. Not a blue shirt, and I didn't care how expensive the blue shirt was. We wore white shirts. We wore a dark suit. I made it simple. Dress shoes had to be polished. If I saw shoes that weren't polished, there were consequences.

Our clients cared about our appearance. Before our sales team had opened their mouths, clients had formed an opinion of who we were, and who we were was a representative of TimeLine Recruiting. In the initial job interview, I spelled out our policies. For example, one of those policies was no facial hair—no moustaches, no goatees, no bushy sideburns. Some of the men went home and shaved just to get the job. Some didn't and weren't offered a position. As for tattoos and piercings, they had to be covered. I had a recruiter with a tattoo on the top of her foot, and if she wore high heels, she had to wear dark stockings to cover the tattoo.

I remember one of my best salesmen, Chris, and I were in the Piper Meridian on the runway preparing for take off to meet a client, and I looked back and noticed Chris didn't have his suit jacket with him. I throttled back and taxied to the hanger, and Chris went to his car and got his jacket.

Uniformity was also crucial. I insisted that every cubicle in the office was set up identically in terms of the physical layout and equipment. I wanted cubicles to be interchangeable. If someone called in sick or was terminated or quit, any recruiter or manager could sit down and know where everything was, from client folders to physician candidate information. I cared less about where the personal pictures hung and more about function and process. I insisted staff store information on our computer database using the same filing and naming conventions.

The Value of Pods

In addition to updating the sales procedures manuals, I added a fair amount of supplementary structure to the recruiting process as well. For example, I formalized our policy of seating new recruiters next to an experienced recruiter with four or more years of experience. This is something we had done intuitively for some time. Now it was policy. I wanted the new recruiters to listen and learn. By hearing the lingo and watching the body language and being next to an enthusiastic and experienced recruiter, new recruiters would learn by proximity. They learned good habits because you don't make it in this business four years or more unless you've created good habits. This proximity approach also taught new employees health care jargon and acronyms. Health care is all about acronyms, and if you don't know the lingo, you can't effectively convince a doctor you know what you're talking about.

Sometimes we matched new and experienced staff based on both experience and personality type. If I had a boisterous recruiter, I'd pair him with another boisterous recruiter. The idea was to build a rapport and let the process of mentoring take place at a personal level. If the pairing didn't work or the production was lower than expected, we'd move new staff around until we found a connection that worked. If I had a woman who was soft-spoken and meek but appeared to have lots of potential, I might put her next to another soft-spoken recruiter who produced stellar results. Voice was only one of the tools recruiters used to find and convince doctors to listen to the opportunity. You didn't have to be loud or pushy. You had to have a range of skills and knowledge plus confidence all working together to produce results.

I was careful how I paired people. Our vice-president of recruiting, Nora, and I spent a lot of time on the pairings This was all part of our pod concept. We arranged our cubicles into pods of five cubicles each. Each pod contained a manager, a very experienced recruiter, two semi-experienced recruiters, and one newbie. The pod formed a recruiting team. The manager in each pod was responsible for training and promoting a culture of excitement and encouragement. The long-range goal was to make or identify another leader. Whom do you see coming up that was going to be the next rock star? What are you doing to solidify their goals? Are you selling the fact that we need more leaders? The company was growing, and we needed more people, but I couldn't hire more people if I didn't have anyone to lead them, and the pod managers understood this.

Everybody always knocks the multi-level marketing model and how these companies grow, but I liked the idea, and I applied it to both my sales and recruiting teams. Both the sales and recruiting staff worked in pods that contained a manager, an experienced salesperson or recruiter, two semi-experienced staff, and one newbie. The advantage of a team like this is that if the team was working well, the staff invariably talked it up with their friends, and those friends often applied for a job because they wanted to be a part of a team. And at each level, success was rewarded with a great commission structure. This is multi-level marketing at its simplest, and it works.

By late 2004, TimeLine was growing faster than we could keep pace. To give some perspective, from 2002 to the end of 2004, our revenue grew by a whopping 164 percent, from $1.1 million to approximately $2.9 million respectively, and our annual growth rate was climbing. One way to maintain enthusiasm at the recruiter level was to make the job fun by hiring friends. TimeLine became a place where friends worked with friends. By the end of 2004, we had eight recruiting teams. This number blossomed to twelve recruiting teams and six sales teams by the end of 2007.

The Right Direction—Inward

About the time I was fattening up our sales and recruiting procedures, I had in my head that if I had well-written policies and good executives and solid support staff in our accounting and direct mail departments, the company would continue to grow without my help. I was wrong, of course. What I learned was that as we took on more clients and placed more doctors, the organization needed even more attention. My executive management team was great. Members of my inner circle were educated, experienced, and committed, but they also needed a visionary who could occasionally step back and look at the organization, the industry, and the economy and make sure we were headed in the right direction.

That person should have been Nora, Beau, or me, yet we were down in the trenches making small day-to-day decisions to keep the organization running. My strategy at that point was counterintuitive. I didn't pull myself out of the mix and focus on long-range strategy; I did just the opposite. I dug in even more. I made myself an indispensable part of the process.

I attended every meeting and got heavily involved with sales and recruiting training. I felt our newest recruiting hires weren't performing as quickly as they might, and one thing I did was create "the pit." The pit was a kind of in-house prospecting pool. Physically, the pit was eight of our smallest cubicles jammed together into a self-contained box. The new recruiters gathered together in this noisy, frenetic, and fun environment and made phone call after phone call trying to locate a doctor for any one of our unfilled searches.

The goal wasn't to give a super-polished pitch but to get a doctor on the phone using any technique you could come up with and then tell him or her about the opportunity. We weren't going for grace and subtlety here. We were aiming for lots and lots of outgoing calls and, if we were lucky, some solid physician contacts. If you made a mistake, so what? Move on. If you said something stupid or froze and couldn't think of what to say at all, so what? Laugh it off and move on.

The goal of the pit was to make so many calls in this very tight environment with all your buddies listening that making the calls became second nature. If you could call a doctor's office from the center of the pit and make a direct pitch to a doctor, you could do it all day long in the comfort of the recruiting floor. The pit was the place people lost their fear. The pit was the place cold calling became fun. It was fast, crazy, impromptu, and a bit of an adrenaline rush when you got a doctor on the phone. And it worked. New recruiters became confident in a matter of days rather than weeks. People began to look forward to cold calling. It was exciting. It was challenging. And in this very tight environment with everyone around you performing the same challenging task, it was fun.

Another benefit of the pit was that doctor contacts were forwarded to a veteran recruiter, which in turn allowed the veteran recruiter to fill searches faster. After a while, veteran recruiters spent their days taking incoming calls or transfers and not cold calling. The veterans got a lot better at closing because they got a chance to do it more often. In all this activity, 2005 was a blur. The sales team kept selling, new recruiters were generating qualified leads, and veteran recruiters were filling searches. We were unstoppable.

I had colleagues in the business calling me asking how we were filling so many searches, and I would tell them. One of my principles was honesty, and that applied to the competition as well. I gave my competitors my recipe, in part because they asked and in part because I knew they would do what my own staff was prone to do if I let them—pick and choose the ingredients they liked and ignore the rest. To illustrate this point, in one of the company-wide training sessions I brought a little propane skillet to work, and I prepared a dish in a shallow pot in front of the employees. The dish had only five ingredients. While I was talking to about eighty employees, I added one ingredient at a time, and I talked about timing and quality and patience. I talked about the smell and the taste. Only I intentionally left out a single key ingredient. I asked for volunteers to taste the dish, and it tasted terrible.

I said I knew it was horrible. I had made it. By leaving out a single key ingredient, I ruined an otherwise delicious gourmet meal. Skip steps in the process and the outcome was disastrous. I told them they did the same thing every day. I gave them the recipe for success, and they picked only the ingredients they liked. They chose the steps that were easy, short-term, or offered immediate feedback. And each time, the sale, the search, or the negotiation fell apart.

The recipe for success in recruiting was like that of any other sales organization. First, you have to be willing to make the investment of time. It's not an eight-to-five job. If you're looking for a job that pays six figures a year, you can't do it by arriving at eight and leaving at five. Second, you have to be willing to take direction, to listen, to be taught, and to soak up learning like a sponge. Third, you must learn to embrace the word *no*. I talked about this in chapter 2 with regard to the concept that believing is contagious. Here I mean it in the most literal sense. A great recruiter falls in love with the word no because he or she understands that enough no's will always lead to a yes. To avoid the no's is to guarantee you won't get a yes. Stop and think about that for a moment. Have you as a business owner or executive given your employees the structure they need? Have you given them the recipe for success? And if the answer is no, why not?

NINE

● ● ● ● ● ● ● ● ●

Pay Attention to the Tires

Do what you're told, and everything will be all right.
—Norman Jewison

Leaders have vision and foresight, they build excellence in others, and they see problems and divine solutions well in advance of a catastrophe. Leaders take action without being told, and at some point, taking action becomes second nature. Before we become that leader, however, each of us must learn to do what we are told. For some of us, that's no easy task. In chapter 4, I described my first days as a school bus driver. Here I tell how I ended that career. About five months after I first set foot in the bus barn, my supervisor, Al, called me into his office and played a tape of a police officer who had just clocked Bus 736, my bus, doing sixty-five miles an hour in a thirty-five mile an hour zone.

I tried to explain myself. The kids fought and threw things. They ran up and down the aisles. They didn't listen, or if they did, it wasn't for long. The more time those kids were on the bus, the more likely something bad would happen. My solution was to zoom from stop to stop and race back to the school as quickly as possible. Occasionally, I tried to slow down, but the chaos on the bus was unrelenting. By driving faster, I was making things safer for everyone. About once a week, after I returned the bus to the barn, Al sat me down and played a new tape of a local cop clocking my speed.

"What do you want me to do?" I asked. "You don't give me a monitor. I can't control these kids, not all of them, not all at once, and not all the time. I'm afraid they're going to start stabbing each other."

Al stood and motioned me to follow. He led me into a large warehouse-sized room I'd never been in. The room was filled with nothing but used tires stacked twenty feet high in long rows. He walked me down one aisle. "Van," he said, "do you see these tires right here? These came off your bus. Five months ago when I hired you, these tires were brand new."

"What are you telling me?"

"I typically get three years out of a set of tires."

"Okay, so I'm tough on tires."

"I've got to let you go."

"Why?"

"Because I can't afford you. Not you and the tires both."

That's when I learned there was a price to pay for getting those kids on and off my bus as quickly as possible. Instead of doing what I was told, I did what I thought was effective, and I lost my job for it. I was told to drive at safe speeds, but I thought the best way to get those kids safely to school was to drive at sixty or better. I wasn't hired to do what I thought was best. I was hired to do what I was told.

Some day I plan to write a book, and I already have a title, *100 Things You Can Do to Keep Your Job*. All one hundred pages will say the same thing: do what you are told.

The Best Employee I Ever Fired

By March 2005, both the marketing and recruiting departments were going strong. The sales department had flourished. Whereas in the past I depended on one or two high producers to make most of the sales, now we had half a dozen. One of the standouts was Charles Price. When Beau was out of the office traveling, Charles kept the in-house sales team focused and moving forward. By April, the sales team had transformed into a highly efficient machine. The team broke one sales record after another and was poised to do it month after month.

I attributed the boost in sales to the additional structure, to a challenge clearly spelled out, to my personal commitment and focus, and to a culture where we worked hard and played hard. It was the playing hard part of that equation that got Charles into trouble. He was a good-looking guy, an aggressive sales person, and a go-getter like I had never seen. From the moment he started, he set the place on fire. Charles was so good he brought in business from every corner of the Midwest. And he was a loose cannon.

We typically traveled for sales calls in pairs, and the staff who traveled with Charles said he had a habit of embarrassing them or himself when he drank too much. Wining and dining a client at lunch or dinner were common, but Charles did it with a little too much gusto. He told racy jokes, or he might have one too many drinks and say something off the wall. I don't think there was any real harm done, but the sales staff didn't like it, and it was hard to tell what a client might think. Right or wrong, I let the entertaining and minor faux pas slide and didn't pay much attention.

I did take action, however, when I found out Charles was bad-mouthing me to other sales staff. One after another, a sales rep would come in and tell me some crazy thing Charles had said about me or the company. The bottom line was that he wasn't a loyal employee, and I had had enough with unfaithful employees. When I hired Charles, I'd begun requiring employees to sign a non-compete agreement. According to the rumors, he was angry at signing his non-compete agreement because he thought he could make more money working for a competitor. Charles was an exceptional salesman, and he was breaking all sorts of sales records. But he wasn't the bedrock of this organization or any other.

Not long after, Beau called and said he had gotten a call from one of his sales reps traveling with Charles. They were somewhere in backwoods Illinois when, according to the caller, Charles had a breakdown and wasn't making any sense. I telephoned Charles and got his voice mail. I left a message asking him to call me immediately. He didn't call. An hour later I called again and again, and I finally got him on the phone.

"Charles, what's going on?" I asked.

He was irate for reasons I still didn't understand. "I hate this company," he shouted. "And I can't stand you." I asked what I could do to help. He wanted more money, a promotion, and shouted a long list of ridiculous demands at me. We talked for several minutes. Our conversation was stilted, and Charles wasn't making any sense.

"I planned to give you the weekend to pull it together," I said, "but I don't think that's in the best interest of the company. Effective immediately, you're fired."

Even with Charles's non-compete agreement in place, he went to work for a competing recruiting firm. TimeLine was on a roll, and I didn't want Charles to impede our progress by stealing our clients. I filed a lawsuit alleging that he had breeched his non-compete agreement.

I tried to be reasonable with Charles. My attorney assured me our case was airtight, yet I nonetheless wanted to avoid a costly court battle. I offered a settlement, but Charles and his attorney simply would not budge. I had my own reasons for being stubborn and forging ahead. I didn't want to set a precedent that TimeLine's non-compete agreements wouldn't be enforced.

Charles's leading argument was that it wasn't his signature on the non-compete agreement. We produced several company documents with his signature on them, one after another, and Charles agreed all the signatures were his except the one on the non-compete agreement. The judge looked at all the signatures and at the non-compete agreement and commented that they looked pretty close.

Prior to trial, Charles's attorney had requested all kinds of company records: everything from phone records and billing statements to sensitive company documents and mail campaign receipts. The issues, it turned out, were discrepancies in our direct mail campaign invoices. Each month we sent out thousands of direct mail letters to doctors and hospitals advertising TimeLine Recruiting services. Charles's contention was that I had failed to send at least one of these mail campaigns and in doing so prevented him from doing his job. In short, if true, not sending mail we agreed to made me look bad and Charles look good.

I took the stand, and Charles's attorney showed me an invoice where we had billed the client for several mail campaigns for the same physician specialty. One of the campaigns showed a zero balance, presumably meaning we didn't send any mail for that particular campaign. The attorney asked me about it, and I explained we could send as many as one hundred campaigns in a month. I didn't oversee them all, and I couldn't remember this specific campaign. At best, I looked as though I had lax quality controls in place. At worst, I came off as if I was hiding something. Then I remembered a plausible answer. I told the attorney and the judge that we occasionally sent a bulk of mail for an upset client who wasn't getting the results anticipated. Kind of like going to a restaurant where your dish is not acceptable and the server comps it for you to insure your return to the establishment. If for whatever reason we had gotten crosswise with a client, we offered to save the client some money by sending a month's worth of mail for a specific search at no cost. The attorney had nowhere to go with his line of questioning, and it appeared that was all he had.

The judge ruled in our favor and further restricted Charles from working for any recruiting company in the entire country for two years. If he breached the ruling, the judge said Charles would be in contempt of court and the penalty would be severe given that Charles had so flagrantly lied.

Divvying Up the Territory

With the Charles lawsuit behind me and the momentum still with us, I made a conscious decision to transform TimeLine from a boutique recruiting company into a major player. To make that happen, I needed bodies. I needed lots of recruiters smiling and dialing, and I needed more sales staff. At that time, each salesperson was assigned a massive multi-state territory. These territories, I realized, were far too big to penetrate effectively. Because of the size of the territories, my sales team was cherry picking: going after easy accounts in larger communities or making repeat calls on existing clients. They were not doing what they were told, which was to tackle untouched areas of their territories in order to land new accounts. They didn't listen to me or Beau, my vice-president of sales, because they didn't have to: the territories were large enough that the sales team worked on the easy accounts first, and there was no end, it seemed, to the number of easy accounts.

I hired eight new sales people over the next five months. At the same time, I rearranged the sales territories. Where once each salesperson had five, six, or even seven states to cover, he or she now had two. In effect, I forced them to get intimate with all of the health care facilities and administrators in their territory. I taught them our sales approach, and I told them to go out there and cultivate those relationships.

Hiring so many new sales staff at once was a gamble. It was painful financially. I couldn't afford it, but I did it anyway. I crunched the numbers, and I ran though a wide range of scenarios regarding potential revenue and expenses, training time, sales, search fallout, number of filled searches, employee turnover, the economy, and any other criteria I could come up with that might affect my business in some way. On paper, the hiring made sense. My biggest concern was getting our sales revenue well above our sales costs as quickly as possible.

Sales for physician recruiting services included heavy phone work and extensive travel each month. The sales staff had to get face-to-face with the CEO or other decision makers. They hopped a plane, rented a car, and drove for hours from hospital to hospital and town to town. And each time any one salesperson took a trip, I got what amounted to a $2,000 travel bill. At one point, I had over twenty sales staff traveling twice a month, which amounted to $80,000 in travel expenses per month.

Most of our business came from smaller towns and communities with a single hospital. Small towns across the Midwest were hours apart, and the best we could hope for were four meetings throughout the day and a dinner meeting. The sales staff would return after a week of travel, spend the next week planning their next trip and closing on any new business they had acquired, and travel the following week.

The sales process was grueling, and I made it even tougher by pushing the staff even harder. We had daily calls where I kept track of each salesperson's location, meeting results, sales leads, and travel time. No matter the results, I encouraged them to keep moving. I was, in effect, creating the same environment

I had created with the recruiters working in "the pit." I wanted to keep the sales staff so busy they couldn't think. Or, at least, I didn't want them thinking too much about each call or about small mistakes they had made or dwelling on the number of no, thank you's they had to hear before they heard a yes.

I wanted enthusiasm and activity and movement. Make a solid sales call, tell the prospect about our product, listen to feedback, and then hit the road. It wasn't easy, and I got plenty of push-back from my staff. The clients weren't interested, they complained, and scheduling meetings in multiple towns was tough. Occasionally salespeople grumbled they were simply worn out. And with each protest, I listened, and then I said to do what you're told. I had been selling hospitals for years, and I knew it would work. Stick to the plan and trust me.

The result of all this activity was better than anyone expected. Business started rolling in, and I kicked myself for not implementing a more aggressive sales strategy sooner. It was hard to tell if the primary driver was smaller territories, a stronger sales pitch, more meetings per day, or the attention Beau and I paid to the sales staff. The bottom line was that our sales team brought in more business in a shorter time frame than at any point in our company history. This fast-paced approach allowed the sales staff to meet more people, improve their message, and make the pitch with greater confidence all because they were making the pitch more often and therefore got very good in a matter of weeks rather than months.

At the same time, we began to feel and act like a large company. We dropped the "we are small and can give you personal attention" vocabulary in exchange for "we are one of the biggest and best agencies in the Midwest." In fact, we were not large in terms of filled searches or annual revenue. We just felt large. I knew if we projected ourselves as one of a handful of large companies in the physician recruiting industry, it wouldn't be long before we became one. Sure enough, the approach was a success. By the end of 2005, our revenue had jumped 31 percent over the previous year to $3.9 million.

"Do as You Are Told" Revisited

What got me into financial trouble was my willingness to take risks. I invested in companies I had no business investing in. I took on partners who looked and talked like a million bucks but who didn't execute. I neglected to pay taxes and ignored the consequences as long as possible. I hired key staff and trusted them to be loyal with little or no rationale for that trust. I took on sales staff with personal problems and believed the problems could be overcome with hard work. Each of these experiences was a risk I undertook, and all of them failed. Yet it was my ability to take risks, assess the outcomes, and then move forward that allowed me to grow the company as quickly as I had. The attitude that got me into trouble was the same attitude that would eventually lead to my success: my ability to take risks.

One of the risks of selling all that new business was that we now had to fill all those searches. The company earned substantial revenues from the monthly professional fees, yet our core mission was to locate doctors and fill searches. Filling that many searches meant having the appropriate number of recruiting staff, ensuring they were well trained, and keeping the troops motivated. We had the numbers in place, yet much of the staff was new or had been with us for less than a year. Training was an issue. As for motivation, the solution to making a large team of new recruiters most effective was to make sure we all had the same road map.

Each of us has a vision of who we are and who we want to be. That vision can be straightforward: "I am a recruiter today and want to be the vice-president of recruiting in the future." Or the vision can be more short term: "I'm the guy who drives an old beat up truck today and want to be a guy who drives a Lexus tomorrow." With regard to my employees, whatever the vision, it's important that TimeLine help support that vision.

If an employee's vision is to work four-hour days and leave at noon, that's not going to succeed because TimeLine can't support that vision. On the contrary, I needed a building full of recruiters whose vision was so large they were willing to put in long days of hard work to make it come true.

One way to go about inspiring people was to talk with each person individually and ask what got each one excited, what people, places, things, activities, and ideas motivated him or her. A better approach for a large organization like TimeLine was to share my vision for the company and invite each employee to join me on the journey, to offer a challenge and invite people to help me and the company to meet that challenge.

In a way, this approach avoided a collision of promised lands. My job was to merge my employees' vision with my professional vision and in doing so create an environment where we supported each other. What I did was give employees a conceptual road map. This road map defined the company promised land. I spelled out our strategy in terms of tangible metrics like revenue growth and filled searches, and I also talked about less tangible drivers like momentum, competence, ideas, and energy. I described the TimeLine of the future and included unique qualities such as energy and innovation, both of which I believed were essential to sustainable growth. Without these intangibles, a recruiting company was reduced to people working the phones for eight hours a day, and we were much more than that.

My goal was to make the intangibles a vital part of how employees thought about TimeLine. If I could do that, I would have a company where culture, values, and teamwork were on par with revenue and expenses, and I could keep people motivated for years. In company meetings, I routinely talked about the road map, about our intangible assets, brand, goodwill, value, and keeping our word to the organizations who entrusted us with their recruiting business.

The road map was a conceptual framework and a new way of thinking about the company. It took time to sink in. At some point, I had buy-in from my senior management team and not long after from the sales and recruiting teams. The big question was how we planned to translate the road map into action. What exactly, employees wanted to know, could they do to help us get to the promised land. What were the steps in the process that guaranteed success?

Changing a company culture doesn't happen overnight. Even a small change like setting sights a bit higher, adjusting mission, or retooling vision can take months and years to actualize. To speed up the process, over the next several months, I held a series of meetings, and in each meeting, I said basically the same thing. I offered the road map, and in exchange all I asked of employees was to do what they were told. Be willing to make an investment in time, take direction, listen, and learn. Read and internalize the company procedures, know your job duties, and strive to reach your individual goals. If they did exactly what they were told, we would soon become the vision I described.

I became vigilant about keeping everyone to the road map. If I happened to hear a recruiter on the phone presenting an opportunity to a physician and the recruiter wasn't selling the opportunity the way we had taught, I made a point of talking with the recruiter after the call. I invited the recruiter to my office, and we engaged in some one-on-one training. Again, the change didn't happen overnight. I taught, lectured, and cajoled. I held firm that any deviation from our fundamental recruiting process was never acceptable. Each time I invited an employee to my office, I said again that I knew how to get us there and that was to follow the road map.

I had lots of employees, especially new employees, who believed in a better way. And each time employees got off the path, I had to reel them in and in many cases did the reeling myself. In this way, the company president and CEO was walking the walk. I didn't order people to follow procedure; I preached it. I believed it. And if an employee stopped following the plan, I sat him or her down and retrained. I asked employees to explain to me why their way was better. Normally they couldn't put it into words while I always had thirty reasons to do it my way. Whatever the process—sourcing, cold calling, presenting, screening, qualifying, or closing—I'd done it for over twenty years, and I knew what worked.

The biggest challenge for new recruiters was displaying confidence when they had none. Recruiters had to be poised and self-assured on the phone with a doctor or hospital administrator. When going over the terms of the employment agreement or negotiating compensation, doctors wanted to know we understood what we were talking about. They didn't want a kid on the other end of the phone; they wanted an expert.

What this really meant was that my young recruiters had to grow into mature recruiters and do it fast. If you were a recruiter, you had to believe in yourself, and until that happened, I asked each of them to believe in me, believe in my words, believe in the training, and believe in the process. I would often sit down with a new recruiter and say, "I know you're only twenty-three, just out of college, and you've never talked to professionals at this level. I know you're scared, but you have a unique skill these people don't. You know how to recruit doctors." The goal was to get recruiters to trust themselves enough to project their voices, ask questions, and give directions. If they did that on enough calls, genuine confidence soon followed.

We began filling searches, and one victory led to another. We billed our clients for filled searches, and our accounts receivables began to grow. We didn't immediately get a boost in cash, but we occasionally had weeks when a big pile of cash rolled in. Cash flow was still erratic and very frustrating. In the end, all the hard work paid off. Revenue improved month after month and continued to climb well into the following year. By the end of 2006, our revenues had grown over the previous year by 21 percent to $4.6 million. Perpetually retaining staff and retooling the company was hard and stressful work. It took time before our recruiting successes caught up with our sales successes, but eventually they did, and it was hard to imagine another year filled with so much positive change. Little did I know what lay ahead.

TEN

● ● ● ● ● ● ● ● ●

Hold 'Em or Fold 'Em?

Believe it or not, quitting is often a great strategy,
a smart way to manage your life and your career.
                                            —*Seth Godin*

Wisdom can mean understanding when to stick and when to quit. I had built a very successful recruiting company, we had strong revenue growth, and I hoped things would get even better. Why then did I entertain the possibility of selling? Back in late 2005, as I was frantically hiring and training sales and recruiting staff, I got a voice mail from Rob Laufer. Rob represented a large health care recruiting company who expressed an interest in purchasing a successful physician recruiting company.

At first, I didn't give Rob's message a second thought. Then, without knowing it, I mulled over the events of the previous year—the country's economic growth had crashed at year's end to the slowest pace in three years, consumer spending was down, auto sales collapsed, interest rates were up, and in August, Hurricane Katrina hit New Orleans, damaging levees and flooding the city. What impact these collective forces might have on physician recruiting was anybody's guess. As I thought about it, I had other issues to contend with. I hadn't given any real thought to succession or creating a viable estate for Julie and Reagan if something happened to me. I was constantly under threat from competitors with loads of cash. And at times, I was simply exhausted.

I got the call from Rob as Julie and I were on our way out of town. I told her about the voice mail. She laughed it off.

"You're not selling, are you?"

"No, I'm not selling."

"That's what I thought." She looked at me and did that thing with her eyebrows.

"I'm not. Really."

"I can hear it in your voice."

"I'm not selling."

About a week later, I got an e-mail from Rob explaining it was in my best interest to talk. He faxed a confidentiality agreement, I signed it and faxed it back, and we talked for the next forty-five minutes. Rob got me talking about the company, and mostly I talked about the staff. I said one of the things that kept me here was that I loved my people. I loved my management team, and I didn't know what I'd do without them around me. Whoever this company was, if he was looking for a company to gobble up and then cut expenses by gutting the staff, I wasn't interested.

We finally talked money, and I told Rob the number I wanted for TimeLine. I even remember telling him the company might not be worth that number but that it was the only number I would entertain. If the company he represented didn't have any interest at that price, then we should not waste each other's time. "If your buyers don't have the ability to write that check, we don't have a deal," I said. I told him I didn't want certificates, stock, or options; I wanted the number in hard cash deposited into my bank account. Rob said that wasn't a problem. He quickly told me this organization had the ability to write a check as long as they saw the value.

At the time, I carried about a million dollars in debt—a line of credit, business and personal credit cards, refunds to clients, taxes, and a handful of other obligations that tugged at me like a hulking, rusty anvil. In addition to debt, I'd made promises to a few people. Prior to starting TimeLine, when I had just finished college, I'd borrowed $30,000 from my father to go to flight school. He didn't have any money, but of course, back then I didn't know he didn't have any money, and I assumed he could make things happen, which he did. After I started the company, he called one day and said to forget about the debt, just give him 5 percent ownership in TimeLine.

"What if the business crumbles in a few months, or what if I never sell?"

"Then you don't owe me a thing."

Neither of us, it seemed, considered that the business might some day be worth something. If I did get the number I wanted, my father would walk away with a large chunk of money. I had received other tentative offers to sell over the years, and at one point, I had promised Beau and Nora that if I did sell, I'd write each of them a check for $100,000. Let's not forget the broker's fee of 5 percent. After all these deductions, whatever was left would be taxed at about 40 percent, and I'd be left with a healthy payday.

I was dreaming big at that point. I owned a lake house with a mortgage of just over $300,000, and I envisioned paying off the loan. In fact, in a matter of days, I had mentally spent every penny of the purchase price I had in mind.

I reluctantly talked to Julie and told her about my conversation with Rob. She wasn't surprised, but she was ambivalent about the sale. She wasn't the type to go gaga over big numbers, and I think she was perfectly content with the way things were. I had mixed emotions yet kept reminding myself that if I got my price, I'd stick to my word and not back out. I could make us debt free overnight and still put some money in the bank. Then I could do something else for a living, something that didn't require a lot of staff. Julie's question was what that something else might be.

I was forty-three at the time, young and full of energy. One of the things I wanted was to speak for a living. A piece of my heart longed to become a professional inspirational speaker. I also had visions of writing a book, and I wanted to own a restaurant. I still had plenty of dreams outside of TimeLine, and the more I thought about it, the better I liked the idea of selling.

The Suitor Revealed

Rob finally gave me the name of the potential buyer, Maxim Healthcare Services, a privately owned company headquartered in Columbia, Maryland, with annual revenues of nearly $260 million and twenty-six thousand employees. Rob planned several meetings with Maxim executives, and the first thing that struck me was how quickly the Maxim executives and I began forging relationships.

My primary question was whether Maxim would take good care of my company. I flew out to Columbia, Maryland, and met with Maxim president Stuart Buss. Stuart came across as a solid, earnest guy and a man I could trust. He had integrity and a genuine concern for the recruiting business. He told me repeatedly that if this thing did end in a sale, he would take care of my employees, and he wanted me to stay on board for several years. In turn, I told him that as long as things went well and I was making money for the company, I'd be happy to stay. The way Stuart presented the acquisition, not much would change except, of course, that after the sale, TimeLine would have more financial, marketing, and advertising resources backing the organization than I could imagine.

After I spoke with Stuart, he sent a couple of accountants back to my office in Columbia, Missouri, and they began the long process of evaluating the company for a potential acquisition. At that point, I hadn't told my staff about a possible sale. If I mentioned Maxim at all, it was in reference to an accounting firm auditing our operations. The Maxim staff looked at our facilities, staff, policies and procedures, quality controls, and accounting records. Then they flew home to Baltimore, and we engaged in a flurry of phone calls. At some point, we both agreed to take the negotiations to the next level, and they asked for copies of my financial records.

Their accounting staff started breaking down the numbers. They distilled every expense, every purchase, and every accounting line item to determine each service or product, what we did with it, and why it was necessary to the business. Some items weren't necessary to the business. My $130,000 Mercedes Benz S500 and Julie's Chevy Suburban were two good examples. Many of the expenses the accountants decided were frivolous or at best not critical to our business. For example, I bought season tickets to the University of Missouri basketball games. I used the tickets as giveaways for contests or gave them to clients who visited us in Columbia. I bought season college football tickets and made donations to the University of Missouri Athletic Department. I routinely participated in charity auctions. All of this wasn't, strictly speaking, a critical business expense. I got what seemed like fifteen phone calls a day asking questions about our expenses. Then they got really serious.

The accountants liked what they saw and asked me to enter into a formal due diligence process. I agreed, and Maxim sent in a team of multiple accounting and acquisition specialists to set up shop in our office for almost a week or more and review all of our accounting records down to the smallest receipt. They sat down with our accountant and bookkeeper and asked them to prove every payment of income and every expense. It was a painful process, and by that point, they had been gathering data for almost eight weeks. The exercise was to understand our revenue and expenses well enough to value the business. They were trying to come up with a number. I didn't care how they arrived at the number because I wasn't selling for a penny less than the number I had in my mind, not necessarily because that was the value but because selling wasn't worth it for less than the number.

Eventually the accountants finished their due diligence and returned to Columbia, Maryland, to compile the data. They gathered up the information and created a fancy report and delivered it to the decision makers at Maxim. A key piece of the report listed our annual earnings before interest, taxes, depreciation, and amortization (EBITDA) as revised by the accountants. There are many ways to value a business, but one of the most common is to determine an accurate EBITDA and apply a multiplier consistent with the industry. The multiplier in the recruiting industry could be five, six, seven, or even higher. EBITDA valuations eliminate the effects of financing and accounting decisions and ignore any debt interest. This approach focused on the health of the company's sales and was a good measure for evaluating profitability.

In our case, our most recent annual EBITDA was over a million, which helped me know which multiplier I needed to arrive at the number I wanted. The EBITDA number is what it is. It doesn't change. The multiplier, on the other hand, wasn't cast in stone but a rule of thumb based on the economy, company revenue potential, client retention, and a host of other factors. Maxim approached me with a multiplier that got my number where it needed to be. This was a grueling negotiation, and at some point, I lost my cool and suggested the Maxim team go refigure the numbers because until they came up with a multiplier that met my asking price, we didn't have a deal.

Rob, my broker, called and said Maxim was pulling out of the deal. As a last minute compromise, he said they were willing to boost the multiplier to a number that valued the company at about $800,000 less than I wanted. I said, "No deal." I told him to figure out a way to reach my asking price and, once he did that, to give me a call. A day later, he called back. Maxim was finally prepared to write the check I needed to be comfortable with the sale of my baby.

If things weren't complicated enough, once we agreed on a price, they only got worse. I had to hire an acquisition attorney out of Kansas City, Greg Yowell, and together with my CPA, Dale Young, and my corporate counsel, Rob Caldwell, those three guys did most of the detail contract work. My tab for these three was well over $100,000, and they earned it because they pulled a lot of all-nighters in the process.

Once Maxim president Stuart Buss had given his blessing to the deal, my main contact was Julian Mitchell. Julian was a good guy, and he called me from time to time to chat and ask how things were going. Our conversations addressed transitional issues, for example, changing over the phone system to match Maxim's phone system. Julian pointed out that I was paying $40,000 a year to a private marketing company that would no longer be needed because Maxim had a team at the home office to do the job. One of the least pleasant aspects of the acquisition was identifying staff redundancies in our support services, positions like bookkeeping and mail handling. Julian identified TimeLine staff that wouldn't be needed, and we talked for hours about where we might use the staff in other positions and how we would transition the job functions to Maxim's corporate office.

One of our issues was my staying with the company after the acquisition. Greg Yowell, my acquisition attorney, suggested a formal earn-out agreement. I didn't know what that meant. He explained that we would draft an agreement

that spelled out my compensation over the next several years.
If the company hit our budgeted numbers over the next two,
three, or more years, for example, Greg suggested I get an
opportunity for a bonus. It sounded good, and I told Greg to
begin negotiations. Greg put the earn-out agreement together,
and then the next thing I knew, I had a document that spelled
out my compensation in black and white. I'd get the number I
requested originally and an opportunity to earn an additional
$2 million over the next two years—a generous base salary
with an even more aggressive plan plus stock options. If I hit
the earn-out targets, I would have effectively sold TimeLine
for a number well in excess of the original number I had in
my mind.

In March 2006, we closed the sale. I received 80 percent
of the sales price when the deal closed and the remaining 20
percent a year later, contingent on my hitting a predetermined
EBITDA number, which we did. The first year following the
sale, we increased revenue from $4.2 million to $6.8 million.
By year-end 2007, revenue jumped again to $7.7 million. In six
short years, I had grown a company from nothing to one of the
darlings of the recruiting industry.

After the Sale

In May 2006, two months after the sale, I reflected on the
events of the previous six months. From the moment I was
approached by Rob Laufer to the final signing, I experienced
a roller coaster of emotions as never before in my life. There
wasn't a moment I didn't believe the deal would fall apart. There
were so many moving parts to the negotiation that I was often
overwhelmed. As some point, I'd mentally made the transition
to selling the company, and I'm not sure what I would have
done had the sale tanked. In the end, Maxim treated me fairly.
I was able to come to work, do what I did best, and go home

without the massive financial responsibilities I had carried around for the past several years. And I loved it.

I left the company in September 2008, two years after the sale, and the same year we hit $11 million in revenue. The lesson was that it was the right time to quit, and I did it successfully. Knowing when to quit is always a challenge. In this case, my decision was strategic and not reactive. I wasn't running away from the challenge, far from it; I had faced the obstacles of growing my business—the crushing cash flow issues, my own bad decisions, employee debacles, and fierce competition from giants in the industry—and I was rewarded for my efforts in the marketplace.

Clients recognized our confidence and awarded us new search contracts. Industry leaders like Maxim Healthcare Services took notice. Maxim recognized our value and the value to the organization and made me an offer. I took the offer because it was the right time to quit. I'd pushed through those first few difficult years and become stronger and more insightful. I learned the hard way to let go of businesses and interests outside my core strengths and my core business. Only by focusing on a single business in a single location with a singular passion did I free resources of time, energy, and money to grow TimeLine Recruiting as quickly as I did. By quitting these other activities, I learned to master one. I encourage you to do the same.

EPILOGUE

● ● ● ● ● ● ● ● ● ●

The Jizzle Wizzle Effect

Since selling my company in March 2006, the question I hear most often is why my company sold when it clearly wasn't the most profitable, the best managed, or even a leader in its market. Why was my company worth millions when it didn't have any innovative products or services, no stellar sales people, no large national clients, no earth shattering vision, and a location in the little town of Columbia, Missouri? What enabled me to position TimeLine Recruiting at the top of the list of companies to acquire? Put another way, why did the leading company in the recruiting industry come seeking me?

I believe the answer is simple. After months of trying to come up with some inspirational and straightforward answer to describe my business success, I concluded that TimeLine Recruiting had that *it* factor, by which I mean that magical combination of both tangibles and intangibles that make some organizations prosper year after year.

When was the last time you opened a dictionary and looked up the word *it*? Recently I did just that and here's what I found: It can be used as a subject or an indirect object of a verb or as an object of a preposition in reference to a lifeless thing. It can be used as the subject of an impersonal verb or as the subject or object of a verb, or it can refer to an explicit or implicit state of affairs or circumstances. The bottom line is that it has many meanings and none of them, to my way of thinking, help us understand the true power of this little word.

For decades, business thinkers and writers have been trying to pinpoint the key driver to business success, the it of business and management greatness. Possible sources include celebrity leadership, creative compensation schemes, breakthrough business strategies, narrow product focus and niche marketing, use of innovative technologies, managing change, and choosing the right industry. I think the key to building a sustainable and highly valuable business is simpler than that.

I call it the Jizzle Wizzle Effect.

The Jizzle Wizzle Effect is a combination of many things: honesty, awareness, enthusiasm, quality, responsibility, structure, integrity, and many other things I talked about in this book. When I interviewed job applicants, for example, if I didn't believe they were open to the excitement and spirit of the Jizzle Wizzle virus, if I didn't believe they would wake up each day and strive to gain, maintain, and retain the Jizzle Wizzle, they were never invited to join the company. My approach may sound a bit soft and fuzzy, but it's not. I'll admit understanding the Jizzle Wizzle Effect can be a bit like getting your arms around a cloud, yet there is a surefire way to apply the Jizzle Wizzle Effect in your own business—focus on the principles outlined in this book and apply them to your business in a way that makes most sense to you. Do that, and you too will have the it factor and experience the positive outcomes of the Jizzle Wizzle Effect.

Rags to Wishes **Key Points**

- **Principle 1:** Flagrant Honesty—The word *flagrant* usually applies to errors, as in "a flagrant mistake," but it equally applies to any burning and passionate action, like telling the truth.

- **Principle 2:** Believing is Contagious—Belief is the habit of placing trust in yourself and in others. It's more than attitude; it's a conviction in the truth. The power of belief can be applied to many aspects of your business—your mission, strategy, products, services, customers, clients, and ability to market and sell.

- **Principle 3:** Business Simplified—Any good business can be simplified to two actions: making a great product and telling people about it.

- **Principle 4:** Changing Behavior by Giving Options— What do you do when someone in your organization challenges your authority by being insubordinate, by ignoring policy, or by jeopardizing your product quality? My suggestion is to give him options.

- **Principle 5:** Success is Fragile—As a leader you must know everything that's going on within the organization because what you don't know makes you vulnerable. If you make a habit of trusting others to take care of nagging details, to make decisions in the best interest of the organization, and to care about your business as much as you do, you are in for a rude awakening.

- **Principle 6:** Don't Become Outdated—It's easy to forget just how fast the world is changing. Trying to keep pace can be daunting. Remember that just when you think you're the master of something, you're probably outdated.

- **Principle 7:** Leaders Take Responsibility—I would suggest that leadership is more than gathering the most current data and passing out obvious advice based on perfect information. Genuine leadership is about taking responsibility for decisions even when grossly misinformed.

- **Principle 8:** Give Them Structure—How can you impose structure on employees and not stifle creativity and personal drive? One way is to provide an environment where goals are clear and objectives and milestones are well defined. Equally important is understanding the power of limits and restrictions. Far more damaging than too much structure is no structure at all.

- **Principle 9:** Do What You Are Told—Leaders take action without being told, and at some point, taking action becomes second nature. Before we become that leader, however, each of us must learn to do what we are told.

- **Principle 10:** Know When to Quit—Wisdom is understanding when to stick and when to quit. Are there employees, clients, processes, products, and services that would help your company in the long term if you quit them today? If so, now is the time to take action.

From Rags to Wishes is my story of early success followed by lots of failures. And more failures. And more. In fact, the challenges and setbacks never stopped coming. In each case, I worked through the difficult times. I learned from my mistakes, and eventually, I achieved greater success than anything I thought possible. By recounting my story as I have, by sharing both the good times and the bad, my message is that you too have the strength and ingenuity to turn a mediocre business into great one, the leadership to see beyond the current crisis, and the vision to prepare for the next quarter, the next year, or the next decade. Apply some of the principles I outlined in this book, and then apply your own. Write down your principles, test them, execute, and create your own success story. Get started. If I can do it, so can you.

About the Author

Van Allen graduated from college without fanfare, without honors, and without a clue. He finally landed a string of jobs from digging ditches and valet parking to waiting tables, driving a school bus, and everything in between. He earned his Grit and Determination Degree from the School of Hard Knocks, but he never lost his burning desire to grow, develop, and take his personal and professional life to the top.

In 1999, Allen founded Timeline Recruiting, a physician recruiting company. As president and CEO, he built and led one of the largest physician recruiting companies in the country. Van's incessant appetite to take calculated risks made him the industry's gold standard by implementing accountability and integrity through his "Money-back Guarantee." In only seven short years, Timeline Recruiting became the most sought after physician recruiting company and sold to the largest staffing company in the world. Allen truly started with nothing but an idea, a beverage napkin, and a bag of wishes. He attributes all of his success to helping people get what they want out of life. As you read and enjoy some of Van's life lessons, you will expose yourself to the compelling strategies that will help you reach your fullest potential.

Van now spends his time writing, coaching, and entertaining audiences across the country on how everyone can get to the top of their game. If you ever have the opportunity to lend an ear, you won't be disappointed. Van's high energy, excitement, and humor will make you reconsider how you approach life.